PRAGUE

past and present

To my parents, gratefully

MetroBooks

PRAGUE

past and present

Texts
Claudia Sugliano

Graphic design
Anna Galliani

Translation
Neil Frazer Davenport
Studio Traduzioni Vecchia,
Milan

CONTENTS

World copyright © 2001 White Star S.r.l.
Via C. Sassone, 24 - 13100 Vercelli, Italy

This edition published by MetroBooks,
an imprint of Friedman/Fairfax
Publishers, by arrangement with White Star S.r.l.

Library of Congress
Cataloging-in-Publication
Data available
2002 MetroBooks

ISBN 1-58663-496-8
M10987654321

Printed in Italy by Grafedit

For bulk purchases and special sales, please contact:
Friedman/Fairfax Publishers
Attention: Sales Department
230 Fifth Avenue, Suite 700-701
New York, NY 10001
212/685-6610 Fax 212/685-3916

Visit our website:
www.metrobooks.com

1 A great center of attraction in the Old City Square is the astronomic clock. The large upper face shows the year, month and day, the times of sunrise and sunset and of the moon and the movement of the planets.

2/7 This print, dated 1795 by Johann Balzer (1738-1799), depicts the Moldau with the Charles Bridge and the Old City. Then, as now, the river was navigable thanks to the constant ply of ferry boats.

3-6 The Old City gives way to the New City in this splendid panoramic view from north to south. Along the eastern bank of the Moldau, some of the most important monuments of the Bohemian capital may be recognized: the Tower of the Old City Bridge, in the foreground, the cambered roof of the National Theater and,

in the distance, the neo-Gothic spires of the Church of Saints Peter and Paul. On the right may be admired in sequence the bridges linking the two banks of the river: the Charles Bridge, in the foreground, and then the Legil, the Jiraskuv, Palackeho and lastly the red-iron profile of the Zeleznicni.

INTRODUCTION

8-9 On Petrin Hill stretches a large, quiet park, a green oasis offering outstanding views over Prague. The Church of Saint Lawrence, built in 1100 on the site of a pagan temple, was restructured in 1740 in Baroque style.

9 top left The breathtaking beauty of Prague may be truly appreciated from above: the Malá Strana district, with its churches and aristocratic houses, which gently descends towards the Moldau; the river, like a steel ribbon crossed by superb bridges and, on the right bank, the sequence of roofs, domes and bell towers of Staré and Nové Mesto.

9 top right The Petrin Park mantles the hill of the same name to the west of Malá Strana, once a center of worship of the Slav god Perun, from whom its name may come; it is picturesque, above all in spring, with its budding fruit trees, and in summer when it becomes a waving sea of leaves.

"**P**rague, the Golden City," "Magical Prague," "Baroque Prague," perhaps no other European metropolis has so many nicknames. The appeal of Prague, with its riverside position, its series of bridges and its enchanting architecture, has long aroused the desire to capture its essence into a definition. At times, such beauty appears to be inconceivable! When thinking about the Czech capital innumerable mental associations come to mind. Over the centuries, during a long history rich in glorious and dramatic episodes, this city has inspired and provided a propitious home for the arts and culture. Unforgettable are the periods spent here by Mozart, his *Prague Symphony* and his opera *Don Giovanni* which was performed here for the first time on the 29th of October, 1787. You can't help being transported by the notes, as fluent and clear as waves, of Bedrich Smetana's *Vltava* (*The Moldau*), a hymn to the great river.

While the image of Prague is so unitary and perfect, the city itself has instead a diverse and intriguing complexity. Its symbolic center can be identified as the Charles Bridge with its flock of saints, towards which converge the historic quarters and which is dominated from above by the Hrad (the Castle). Passing through the rest of the city, Malá Strana, the "Little Side," Staré Mesto and Nové Mesto, the Old and New Towns, and Josefov, the Jewish quarter, one has the sensation of distinguishing the pieces of a mosaic, each glistening with a particular splendor. Baroque and Rococo Prague is in the Malá Strana quarter on the left bank of the Vltava, immediately after the Charles Bridge, the favorite meeting place of young people from all over the world. Here the Italian-style buildings such as Valdstejnsky palace compete with gilded churches such as St Nicholas's and the Church of the Madonna of Loreto.

8 top The spires of St Vitus's dominate the silhouette of the Castle, atop the Hradcany district, built on the left bank of the Moldau.

8 bottom In Prague, the Old City, seen from above in this panoramic view, is only a part of the extensive old city center. The district, which developed from the 10th century between Hradcany and Vysehrad, in the reign of King Wenceslaus, was surrounded by city walls and in 1235 called a "city" according to German law.

10 left From the enormous ground-floor hall in the Wallenstein Palace, in the Malá Strana gardens, may also be admired the copies of the bronze statues by Adriaan de Vries in the famous garden, including this elegant Eros. The originals, removed by the Swedes during the Thirty Years War, are at Drottnigholm Castle.

10 right The neo-Renaissance dome and façade of the National Museum form the background of the equestrian statue of the patron saint of Bohemia, Saint Wenceslas, to whom the square of the same name is dedicated. The warrior prince is surrounded by four other Czech patron saints: Ludmilla and Procopius, Agnes and Adalbert. The modern monument is the work of J. V. Myslbek (1912-24).

11 left The Cathedral of Saint Vitus, one of the twin spires and the slender Renaissance bell tower of which are highlighted in the picture, was begun in 1344 and completed only between the 19th and 20th centuries.

11 top right The wrought iron gate with the monograms of the Empress Maria Theresa and Joseph II is the official entrance to the Castle. The gate, alongside which waves the national flag, seems to be guarded by two stone giants, copies of the magnificent Baroque statues by I. F. Platzer.

11 center right The Town Hall, situated alongside the old Powder Tower, is the finest monument in Secession style in the city. Under the majestic but light dome, the Prague coat of arms stands out.

11 bottom right The warm shades of brick red of the high roofs and the yellow-ochre of the facades are one of the dominating features in the composite architecture of Prague, which amazes and enchants for the sophistication of its stylistic solutions.

Seen from the bridge, Prague truly appears to be a sea of stone on which Hrad floats, its mainmast the tower of St. Vitus's Cathedral. The castle is a fortified citadel which encloses palaces and gardens, churches and museums. It is reached via the Golden Lane which brings to mind the alchemists of Rudolf II, the emperor fascinated by mysticism and magic who transformed his residence into the "art gallery of Europe." It is said that the alchemists performed mysterious and esoteric experiments in that tiny street.

The broad, placid Vltava, the home of gulls and swans and featuring the island of Kampa, is another of Prague's magical aspects, another facet of its soul. Legends abound in the Bohemian city, and the river too has its own such as the poetic and somewhat melancholic story of the *vodnik*, the man of the waters, the green gentleman who emerges from his domain only by night.

Staromestské Námestí the main square of the Old Town is, along with the Charles Bridge, the beating heart of the city and a place where history can be read like an open book. The monument in the center represents Jan Hus, a priest and great reformer of the Czech church who was burned at the stake at Constance in 1415. The entire square is enclosed as if it were a stage-set by a masterly series of palaces and churches and by the Town Hall, in front of which a crowd of tourists and passers-by gathers as the hours are struck by the astronomical clock. They

are all waiting for the slow procession of the apostles, the skeleton that turn the hourglass and the final, shrill crowing of the cockerel.

A stone's throw from the Old Town stand the synagogues of Jewish Prague. The Jewish quarter is what remains of Europe's largest ghetto in which the writer Franz Kafka walked in a dream, imagining himself to be a ghost of times past. The center of Josefov (as the quarter is known in honor of the emperor Josef II) is the "house of the living," the Old Jewish Cemetery now bustling with tourists within which, in the shade of the elder trees, the stone tombs are crowded in picturesque disorder. Here lies the famous Rabbi Löw, a cabbalist responsible, according to another Prague legend, for the *Golem*, the creature of clay that was supposed to protect the Jews from persecution. Brought to the screen in 1920, the fragile colossus was a kind of prototype for many cinematographic monsters.

The Art Nouveau style is much in evidence around the Town Hall of the Jewish quarter with elegant palaces that in the late 19th century replaced the "insanitary buildings of the ghetto." These palaces feature a riot of coronas and entwining stems, of ethereal dancing figures and peacocks, of stained glass and mosaics, of ceramics and wrought iron.

When one considers that Prague is the capital of a country the president of which, Václav Havel, is an acclaimed writer too, it is easy to comprehend the spirit and character of the city.

12 top The white swans on the Moldau are an essential part of the Prague landscape: in the background the Tower of the Old City and the Charles Bridge, covered in snow.

12-13 In winter the Charles Bridge, with its few passers-by, and the black statues of saints hooded in snow, takes on a new charm.

13 top left In the warm light of sunset the bridges form a sequence on the Moldau, the river which is the star of the opera of the same name by the composer Bedrich Smetana.

13 top right The Old City Square, with its old houses, is transformed when covered in a snowy mantle.

16-17 The dark silhouette of the Church of Saint Mary of Tyn stands out against the background of magnificent buildings. The School of the same name rises in front of the church.

18-19 From the right bank of the Moldau we may enjoy the view of the hill on which stands Malá Strana, crowned by the Castle and the Cathedral of Saint Vitus.

Alongside the faith in the values of liberty and democracy for which he was imprisoned on a number of occasions during the communist regime, Havel conquered his fellow citizens above all for his intellectual charisma. During the heady days of the "Prague Spring," repressed by the Soviet tanks in 1968, Czechoslovakia struggled vainly for freedom; a battle finally won over twenty years later, in 1989, with the "Velvet Revolution," after which a poet was chosen as the country's president. Even revolutions have poetic names in Prague and do not wish the shedding of blood. There was someone, instead, who preferred self-immolation: on the 16th of January, 1969, Jan Palach set himself on fire in Wenceslas Square, becoming a symbol of the struggle and an international hero.

It would, however, be wrong to think of this city in an idealized, abstract manner, enclosing it within the gilded prison of art and beauty. Prague is full of the joy of life, a place in which even the simplest pleasures can be explored to the full. One of these pleasures is beer, and for many citizens of Prague the *pivnice* or beer cellar is almost a second home in which they can meet friends and philosophize over a few glasses of the local brew. Some of these pubs are legendary, such as U Kalicha beloved of the literary hero the Good Soldier Schweik, and one of the oldest, U Fleku, in which a dark beer produced since 1499 is drunk in an atmosphere unchanged for centuries.

Traditions are still alive and deeply felt in the capital city. At Easter colored eggs painted with skill and patience and resembling precious embroideries are exchanged while on the Easter Monday the city takes on the guise of a gay country village with the children playfully whisking the ankles of the women with a plaited reed stick from which colored ribbons hang. This is a never forgotten ritual celebrating the return of spring and the rebirth of nature. On the 5th of December, Saint Nicholas' eve, when in the icy grip of winter the city's architecture is transformed by a mantle of snow, angels and devils roam, distributing gifts and sweets to the children. Such figures are at home in the setting of Prague which for centuries has had a strong theatrical vocation. It is no coincidence that craft shops often offer puppets, as this form of theater, at once popular, immediate, grotesque and symbolic, has always had a strong following here. Theaters famous throughout the world for having successfully combined tradition and innovation have flourished in the city and fantasy, dreams and a surrealist and poetic imagination have always helped the citizens of Prague even in the most difficult moments.

Finding a satisfactory definition for Prague is perhaps impossible, one has to take it as it comes and entrust oneself to its magic. For Prague truly is a magical city.

Hradčany
(Castello)

Malá Strana
(Città Piccola)

LORETANSKA

NERUDOVA

MOLDAVA

Staré Město
(Città Vecchia)
Josefov

Nové Město
(Città Nuova)

PARIZSKA

KARLOVA

CELETNA

NA PRIKOPE

VÁCLAVSKÉ NAMĚSTÍ

NÁRODNÍ

SMETANOVO NABREZI

MASARICOVO NABREZI

PRAGUE,
CRADLE OF BOHEMIA

The birth of Prague is associated with a wholly female legend. It is said that Princess Libuse, the beautiful and emancipated descendant of the patriarch Cech, having realized that her subjects no longer wanted to be governed by a woman, chose as her husband a ploughman by the name of Premysl. She then convinced him to found a city on the banks of the Vltava, prophesying a glorious future symbolized by two golden olive trees, the tops of which would rise as far as the Seventh heaven, shining over the whole world. According to this version, the original nucleus of Prague — a name that may derive from the world *prah* i.e. ford or door — rose around 700 AD on the right bank of the Vltava and was called Vysehrad. Historians instead set the date around 880-890, when the Slav princes of the Premyslid dynasty erected a fortress in that site of great strategic importance.

The castle (*hrad*) became the home of Prince Borivoj and his wife Ludmilla who, in 874, had been baptized by Bishop Methodius (who, with his brother Cyril, introduced Christianity). Borivoj built Prague's first church dedicated to the Virgin Mary, while around 920 his son Vratislav founded the basilica of St. George and, in 925, his grandson Wenceslas (921-935) began work on the Rotunda of St. Vitus where today stands the chapel dedicated to him. These were years of fierce internecine struggle: Ludmilla, Borivoj's widow, was assassinated, the same fate awaiting her grandson Wenceslas, murdered on the orders of his brother and successor Boleslav. Ludmilla and Wenceslas were the first Bohemian saints with Wenceslas becoming the patron saint of the country. In 973 Boleslav II (972-999, known as "the Devoted," obtained the authorization to found a bishopric in Prague. In spite of the princes' faith, the majority of their subjects were still devoted to pagan rituals and Bishop Vojtech (Adalbert the Saint), twice fled to Rome. But the Church played an important role in the Bohemian state that was unified with the conquest of Libice castle by the Premyslids in 995.

20 top Vitezlav Karel's painting in Art Nouveau style depicts the wise Libuse, the legendary figure of the Slav princess, daughter of Cech. According to the oldest Bohemian chronicle she chose as her husband the humble ploughman Premysl, with whom she founded Prague and the Premyslid dynasty.

20 bottom Boleslao II, called "the Devoted," reigned from 972 to 999 and obtained authorization from the German emperor to create a bishopric in Prague, a city which was still dedicated to pagan practices. The most enlightened figure in this process of Christianization was the Bohemian bishop Vojtech, who founded the Brevnov monastery.

21 Saint Wenceslas, portrayed here in a 16th-century work, is the first saint and patron saint of Bohemia. Ascended to the throne in 921, he contributed greatly to the birth of the nation; he was assassinated in 935 by his brother Boleslao, as he entered the church for morning service.

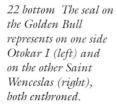

22 bottom The seal on the Golden Bull represents on one side Otokar I (left) and on the other Saint Wenceslas (right), both enthroned.

The kingdom was further consolidated under Vratislav II (1061-1092) who in, 1085, was nominated as King of Bohemia by the Emperor Henry IV. His brother Jaromir claimed the Episcopal throne and, during the struggle between the two, Vratislav moved to Vysehrad, where he built the church dedicated to Saints Peter and Paul, fortified the complex, and declared himself the true representative of Rome.

CLAVSA REX PORTÂ PENETRAT QVE RESPICIT ORTVM

VIRGVLA DE IESSE PCE GOTT SPLENDIDA FLORE

The famous *Vysehrad Codex* with its rich illuminated decorations accompanying selected passages from the gospels was written early in his reign, underlining the importance of the new princely residence. After the deaths of both Jaromir and Vratislav. Hradcany once again became the most important royal residence.

Early in the 12th century the urban nucleus in front of the castle (in 1091, the historiographer Cosmas, author of the first history of Bohemia, mentions the existence of settlements of Jewish merchants in the area and along the Vysehrad road) had moved to the right bank of the Vltava. Of great importance was the construction, 1170 AD, of the first stone bridge over the river, the so-called "Judith Bridge" named in honor Vladislav's wife. Safer than the earlier wooden version, the bridge linked Hradcany

to the market held in the area that was later to become the square of the Old Town. It was Sobeslav I (1125-1140) who made this decision of fundamental importance to the development of Prague, a city with great commercial ambitions. During his reign the capitular hall of the cathedral of Vysehrad was completed. Vladislav II (1140-1172) re-established his residence in the castle, where he had a great palace built, and extended St. Vitus's Cathedral. By this time the city was developing beyond the castle walls and, above all, at Staré Mesto on the right bank of the Vltava, many churches had been built. In 1140 the Premonstratensian monastery of Strahov, subsequently to become famous for its library, and that of St. John were constructed. However, as a result of the struggles and intrigues between the members of the Premyslid dynasty, Vladislav had to give up the throne. Sobeslao II succeeded him in 1173. Otokar I (1197-1230) reinforced the basis of the kingdom by obtaining, in 1198, recognition of the hereditary nature of his title. In the absence of a direct heir, his successor would be elected by the Diet. In 1212 Frederick II confirmed this important dynastic condition in the Golden Bull of Sicily; he also absolved the country from its obligations of vassalage but imposed restrictions on its expansionist ambitions in the Danube area. Prague acquired increasing importance in the Central European context and it was Otokar who founded Malá Strana on the left bank of the Vltava.

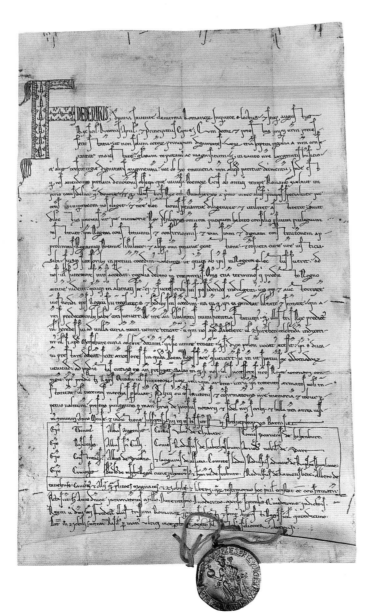

His son Wenceslas I (1230-1253) continued his work, but never succeeded in creating a great Bohemian kingdom. He was responsible for the fortifications around the Old Town and, within the castle walls, the first buildings in the Gothic style. Of these a very few traces remain, such as the foundations and decorated capitals found under the present chancel of St. Vitus's Cathedral. In 1233, Wenceslas' sister Agnes founded and became the first abbess of the Convent of the Poor Clares or St. Agnes, a marvel of early Bohemian Gothic, and also founded a Franciscan monastery that is now lost. Agnes, venerated as one of the patron saints of the country could not be beatified for seven centuries. Only in 1989 did Pope John Paul II canonize her. The long reign of Wenceslas I was disturbed by the revolts of the minor nobility who, under his rule, had lost part of their power, and by the ambitions of his son Otokar. After a flight from Prague following a revolt, he returned to the city and, thanks to the bourgeoisie that had remained faithful to him, was able to quell the rebellion. The ambitious and impatient Otokar II only succeeded his father in 1253 and reigned until 1278. In this twenty-five year period he led his country to unprecedented expansionist victories. During the interregnum of the Holy Roman Empire between 1250 and 1273, the twenty-two-year-old Otokar, thanks to his marriage to the older Margaret, sister of the last Babenberger, had already received

the title of Duke of Austria and of Steirmark, to which, in 1269, he added those of Lord of the Lands of Carinthia and Carniola. He also expanded his kingdom eastwards, towards pagan Prussia. Participating in the crusade of the Teutonic Order, in 1255 the Bohemian sovereign founded Königsberg on the Baltic. However, his imperial ambitions were never realized and, when Rudolf of Hapsburg was elected by the German princes, he refused to restore the territories he had acquired. In 1276, Otokar was obliged to cede all his do-

24-25 *In the Battle of Marchfeld, in 1278, two armies took part made up of thirty thousand men each, led respectively by the Emperor Rudolph I of Hapsburg and by Otokar II of Bohemia. The latter's defeat signified the end of the imperial ambitions of the Premyslid.*

25 bottom This 19th-century engraving depicts the Emperor Rudolph I paying tribute at Marchfeld to the heroism of his adversary Otokar II, unseated and killed with seventeen knife wounds by an Austrian horseman. According to cavalry customs, the Hapsburg remained on the battle field for three days to honor him.

minions, retaining control over Bohemia and Moldovia only. In the *History of Bohemia* by Venceslas Wladiwoj Tomel, published in 1865, the heroic end of this Premyslid king was recounted on the basis of ancient sources. He was killed in 1278 in the cavalry battle fought on the plain of Marchfeld (where eighteen years earlier he had defeated the King of Hungary, Bela IV) between two immense armies of 30,000 men. According to the customs of the country, Rudolf stayed on the battlefield for three days to honor him.

During Otokar II's reign, Prague had achieved the status and beauty of the capital of a great country. A Gothic palace was constructed within the castle and, in 1263, the All Saints Chapel was completely rebuilt. As had occurred during the reign of Vladislav, German merchants continued to arrive in the city and settled in the area to the south of Hradcany where the Gothic church of St. Nicholas was built by the immigrants. The urbanization of the capital was extremely intense in those years and saw the construction of many buildings on the right bank of Vltava such as the New and the Old Synagogues, the only monuments to survive to the present day. In popular memory, the reign of Otokar long remained as an unmatched example of happy and prosperous times. Wenceslas II (1278-1305) was only seven on his father's death and when the Rudolf I gave him his daughter in marriage, thus ensuring a further degree of influence over the young king. One of the positive aspects of his reign was the monetary reform that stabilized savings and reinforced the *groschen*, the coinage minted in Prague from 1300. In

that year, thanks to Hapsburg support, the Bohemian king had obtained the Polish crown, a decision strongly opposed by the Anjevins and the Pope. The reign of his successor, the sixteen-year-old Wenceslas III (1305-1306), was extremely brief as he was assassinated at Olomouc in the struggle over Poland. With Wenceslas III the Premyslid dynasty came to an end and, after a period of regency under Henry of Carinthia and rule under Rudolf III of Hapsburg, John of Luxembourg (1310-1346), son of the German king Henry VII and husband of the younger sister of Wenceslas, Elizabeth aceded to the Bohemian throne. John was above all interested in the politics of the empire, spending long periods away from his kingdom and fighting

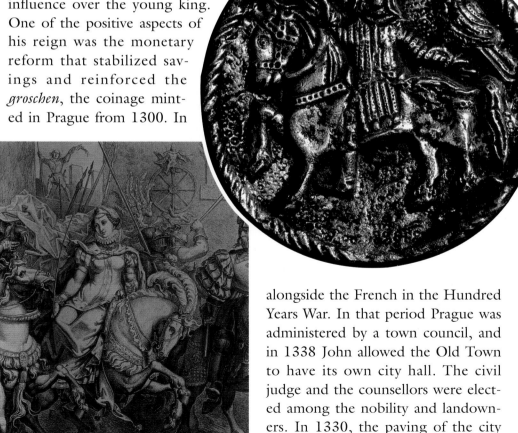

26 Wenceslas II became king as a very young man, after the death of his father Otokar II. The Emperor Rudolph gave him his daughter in marriage and allowed him to take the Polish crown. Wenceslas died after carrying out a great monetary reform.

27 top John II of Luxembourg was the son of the German King Henry VII. He ruled in Bohemia until 1346.

27 center This seal belonged to John of Luxembourg, the King who ruled Bohemia during the Hundred Years War.

27 bottom With the assassination of Wenceslas III, the Premyslid dynasty ended; John of Luxembourg thus came to the Bohemian throne, by marrying the young Premyslid Princess Elizabeth.

alongside the French in the Hundred Years War. In that period Prague was administered by a town council, and in 1338 John allowed the Old Town to have its own city hall. The civil judge and the counsellors were elected among the nobility and landowners. In 1330, the paving of the city streets began at the expense of the wealthy bourgeoisie, and the first public health regulations were published. In the meantime, the castle was gradually falling into ruins.

28 top *The bust of Peter Parler, Charles IV's favorite architect, is found in the triforium of the Cathedral, a veritable gallery of illustrious people. To Parler we also owe the plans for the Charles Bridge and the Old City Bridge Tower, with the statues of Saint Vitus, Charles IV and Wenceslas IV.*

28 bottom *Charles IV appears among bishops in the miniatures of the famous Golden Bull, enforced at the Metz Diet in 1356. With this act the Emperor reconfirmed the indivisibility and independence of the Kingdom of Bohemia, and conferred the right to take part in imperial elections.*

Prague's golden age coincided with the reign of John's successor, his son Wenceslas, who came to the throne of Bohemia as Charles IV. He had chosen this new name on the occasion of his first communion in honor of Charlemagne whom he took as his model. In 1349 Charles was elected as Holy Roman Emperor. Having been educated in Paris by the future Pope Clement VI, and after a stay in Italy, he returned to his homeland in 1333, acting as regent in place of his now blind father. In contrast with John, Charles was enamored of Prague and transferred his imperial court there. He immediately began to embellish the city, restoring the castle and, having obtained the transforma-

tion of the bishopric into an archbishopric in 1344, began the construction of St. Vitus's Cathedral on the remains of the earlier basilica. The edifice was built in the French Gothic style with three naves. After almost ten years, on the death of the architect, Matthieu d'Arras, the work was entrusted to the young already highly experienced Peter Parler of Cologne.

In 1342 an event took place that had grave consequences for the city's trade-based economy: the Judith Bridge collapsed under the weight of huge blocks of ice, cutting off communications between the two banks. In 1357 Charles IV entrusted Parler with the grandiose project of constructing a new bridge, with two towers and sixteen arches over which four pairs of horses could pass. Still today, from the tower of Staré Mesto where he is portrayed as an old man, he overlooks his most famous work, the Charles Bridge.

29 bottom This precious crown, adorned with large gems and the insignia of the Premyslid, was made by Charles IV, who wanted to insert a thorn of the crown of Christ in the sapphire cross. He dedicated it to Saint Wenceslas,

thus attributing to it a spiritual as well as temporal power. Charles IV wore it in 1347 for his coronation as King of Bohemia; two years later at Aachen, he was unanimously proclaimed the German Emperor.

28-29 The picture shows a letter written by Charles IV by his own hand. A cultured king, he surrounded himself with illustrious thinkers and men such as Cola di Rienzo and John of Neumark. The Emperor also wrote his autobiography.

29 top This golden seal belonged to Charles IV, elected Emperor of the Holy Roman Empire in 1349 and instigator of the period of Prague's greatest prosperity, when he transferred the imperial court to the city. He is recalled for the Castle, Cathedral, the Charles Bridge, the Carolina University and the New City.

obtinere· Alius ve
ro princeps aut vir
nobilis ut prefertur
in has nostras leges
temeritatem contine
tens similiter non
vindicatur de feu
dis que a sacro im
perio vel alias obti
net a quocunque: Et
nichilominus dos
prenas premissas se
u decernentes perso
nam incidat corp
so· Qudans aute:
vniuersos princepes
comittes barones
nobiles milites
dicentes ciuitates
quoque: i communita
tes illorum ad pre
standum cuilibet
principi electori v
el eius nuncus pre
fatum conductum

ut predicatur indic
tuncte volumnus et
decernimus obliga
ri· Qdniomnus eor
ciulibt singulares,
editctis i eductore
pregionum i locor
ad iacenncium cuili
lbet magis aptos du
ximus designados
ut statim p sequen
cia plenutis appebt·

nno nax:
irgenu lue
niie sacri
iiii petri archipi

A great builder and urban planner, during Charles IV's reign the face of Prague was transformed. The most significant project, dating from 1348, was that of the construction of the New Town (Nové Mesto), extending from the southeastern area of the Old Town to the river, below the fortress of Vysehrad. In this way the surface area of the capital was doubled. Those willing to move there received a plot of land on which they were to build their home within eighteen months. Whilst echoing the Medieval geometric plan of the Staré Mesto, the New Town was divided into four sectors, three of which were set around the squares holding the markets for horses (present day Wenceslas Square), bulls (present day St. Charles Square, the largest in Europe) and the merchants' street (present day Hybernská). Charles IV, who was himself a writer and an acute intellectual, welcomed scholars and philosophers such as Francesco Petrarca and John of Neumark, his chancellor

and translator from Latin; he was also responsible for the founding, in 1348, of the first university in central Europe. The university, which had a statute similar to that of the one in Paris, initially held classes in various churches and in the Jewish ghetto, but in 1356 it moved to the Karolinum building. This was the year in which, with the famous Golden Bull, Charles IV gave Bohemia the right to participate in imperial elections. When, in 1378, the king died, he left a magnificent city of around 50,000 inhabitants, boasting many churches and monasteries, but also tormented by the conflicts between the inhabitants of the Old Town, the bastion of the bourgeoisie, the aristocracy and the merchants, and those of the New Town, above all craftsmen and shopkeepers. There were also increasingly sharp contrasts between the Czech and German national groups. Charles's son Wenceslas IV (1378-1419), gone down in history as weak and dissolute, received a demanding inheritance. He left the castle in favor of a smaller residence in the Old Town, near the Powder Tower.

During his tormented reign the Hussite crisis broke out. In the Europe of the time there was spreading discontent at the pomp and decadence of the clergy and the monasteries, and the condemnations of such abuses and riches by the English priest and reforming theologian John Wycliff (1320-1384) began to circulate in the University of Prague. In 1391, the Bethlehem Chapel was raised in the Old Town (the present structure was rebuilt in 1950-53), a simple Gothic building where, from 1402, Jan Hus (1369-1415), a priest and professor of philosophy at the university close to Wycliff's doctrines, began to preach. Hus found support above all among the craftsmen and ordinary people to whom he turned in writing his sermons on the walls of the church and by preaching and chanting in the Czech language. Even the emperor Wenceslas was attracted by the ideas of the preacher who called for a return to the purity of the biblical message, partly in the hope that he would be able to draw some personal advantage, re-establishing his own authority at the expense of that of the church. The clergy, however, faced with the loss of their privileges, put up strenuous opposition. In 1409, the dispute spread to the university and was transformed into a nationalistic conflict between Czechs

and Germans. On its foundation the Charles University had been subdivided into four Bohemian, Bavarian, Saxon and Polish "nations." Each one had the right to vote in university affairs and their representatives held in the turn the posts of Chancellor and Rector. Following the Kuttenberg (Kutná Hora) Decree issued by Wenceslas whereby the German nation lost the majority of votes in favor of the Bohemians, the German academics abandoned Prague. In 1410 Jan Hus was excommunicated. To heal the schism a general council was called at Constance in 1414. Hus, determined to defend his ideas with theological arguments, and trusting in Emperor Sigismund's promises of immunity, attended the council. One of the Hus's theses concerned the administering of the Eucharist *sub uiraque specie*, i.e. according to the Bible, in the forms of both bread and

32 This manuscript with the royal seal represents a milestone in the history of Prague: the Decree of Kutná Hora, thanks to which Wenceslas I, in 1409, brought the Carolina University fully under the control of the Czech nation, causing bringing about in fact the drain of all the academics of German nationality. This act was decisive in the field of theological and political dispute which in those years convulsed the Kingdom, Church and the German and Bohemican population, as a consequence of the so-called "Hussite heresy."

wine. The chalice then became the symbol of the Bohemian church and the Hussites were also known as Utraquists. Condemned as a heretic by the Council, Jan Hus was burned at the stake at Constance on the 6th of July, 1415 but his movement had yet to be eradicated. In Prague repression and a series of arrests started, supported by the patrician families who opposed the Hussite social polices. This led to the famous "first defenestration of Prague" of 1419, in which a crowd went to the Town Hall in the Old Town, calling for the liberation of the Hussite prisoners. Having failed, the rebels threw the consuls and seven citizens out of the windows. The consuls were replaced by Hussites and the rebellion extended. In 1418 Hussites scored an important victory: the Czech sinod approved the articles and the symbol of their doctrine.

32-33 This 19th-century work by the English painter Ford Madox Brown represents John Wyclif as he reads his translation of the Bible to John of Gaunt. The writings of the English Reformist priest and reformer, who denounced religious abuses and considered the Pope as "anti-Christ," circulated at the end of the 14th century among Bohemian students, feeding anti-Catholic fervor.

33 top This xylograph taken from the Council Chronicle, published at Augusta in 1483, represents a moment in the Papal ceremony during the Council of Constance (1414-1417), called to end the schism. Jan Hus had gone voluntarily to the Council, taken in by the promise, later broken, of the concession of a safe conduct by the Emperor Sigismund, with the hope of undertaking a serious theological discussion.

33 bottom From the chronicle of Ulrich of Richental, kept in the Prague University Library, comes this miniature - in the photograph - depicting Jan Hus at the stake: the priest is wearing the tall white hat of heresy, with red devils leading souls to Hell.

IOANNES ZISSKA.R.TROCZNOW 3VPERBIÆ 3HIVLET AVARICIÆ CLERICORVM SEVERVS VLTOR.

34 top This portrait of the German School portrays Jan Zizka, the brilliant mercenary who succeeded in transforming the disorderly mass of Hussite rebels into an efficient army and was the first to use *firearms, including a rudimental howitzer, on a large scale. In 1429 he thus succeeded in defeating Sigismund's troops, who were more numerous and better equipped, on Vitkov Hill.*

34 bottom In 1433 Pisanello portrayed King Sigismund, the brother of Wenceslas IV, against whom, immediately after his election, the City of Prague declared war, defeating him at Vitkov. Only after five crusades against the Hussites, in a war-torn and impoverished country, did the sovereign achieve the decisive victory over the Schismatics in the Battle of Lipany in 1434.

Wenceslas IV died in August, 1419, and the city entered into war with his brother and successor King Sigismund. In 1420 the most radical Hussite faction, the so-called "Taborists" (from Mount Tabor, scene of the Transfiguration), whose military leader was one Jan Zizka, a valorous adventurer and inventor of a form of mobile artillery, defeated him at Vitkov. For over two decades the country was lacerated, Sigismund lost five crusades against the Hussites, but

in 1434 they were defeated in the battle of Lipany. The Utraquist George of Podebrady reigned over Bohemia from 1458 to 1471 and, whilst trying to maintain the gains made during the Hussite wars, attempted to restore normality to a Prague stripped and devastated during the long years of religious and social conflict. The population had also declined drastically (now no more than 20,000 inhabitants) and trade, crucial to the city economy, had nearly disappeared. A project was developed that involved more intensive participation in trade with foreign powers, in particular Venice. It was King George who ordered the construction of the tower of the Malá Strana bridge and those of the church of the Madonna of Tyn, the traders' church on the Old Town Square. He was the last Bohemian to wear the crown of Vladislav as he was succeeded by the Pole Wladyslaw II Jagiello (1471-1516), the grandson of Sigismund who from 1490 was also the king of Hungary. During his reign trade was further reinforced, but the city was nonetheless shaken by revolts. Between the 25th and 26th of September, 1483, a second "defenestration" took place (not officially "recorded") when the people stormed the City Hall in the Old Town, throwing from the window the mayor and the spokesman of the Catholics who had re-entered the city thanks to the new king. Following this episode, and in spite of the signing of the Treaty of Kuttenberg which pacified the Utraquist and Catholic parties, Vladislav II left the Old Town to return to the Castle. The reign of his son Louis II Jagiello was brief (1516-1526).

35 bottom The Utraquist George Podebrady was the first Hussite king and the last Bohemian king to wear the crown of Vladislav, from 1458 to 1471. He found a city devastated by religious struggles and social conflict, which he sought to bring back to normality through the setting up of better relations with Rome and an increase in trade.

34-35 Taken from the Nuremberg Chronicle by Hartmann Schedel (1493), this xylograph shows a 15th-century view of Prague, where the nuclei composing it are clearly distinguished: on the left bank of the Moldau, above, the Hradcany district, with the Castle and Gothic Cathedral of Saint Vitus; on the hillside, Malá Strana and, on the opposite bank, linked by the bridge, Staré Mesto. In the foreground the ruins of the Vysehrad may be seen.

36 left The mosaic by Valerio and Vincenzo Zuccherini, taken from a painting by Titian, portrays a thoughtful Ferdinand of Hapsburg, the Catholic king who attempted to bring Prague, dominated by Hussite ideas, back under the influence of the Catholic Church. Although he preferred Vienna to the Bohemian city, he was the first to introduce the ideas of humanism and Italian Renaissance architecture.

36 bottom The Emperor Rudolph II, with a complex, tormented personality, but a passion for art and science, chose Prague instead of Vienna as his official residence, and surrounded himself with the leading artists and scientists of his time. This 17th-century engraving shows him together with the great Johannes Kepler who, summoned to Prague by Tycho Bahe, on the latter's death became court astronomer.

With the choice of the new sovereign, the Austrian Archduke Ferdinand I of Hapsburg (1526-1565), Bohemia determined its future destiny and Prague declined in importance compared with Vienna. However, the new sovereign introduced humanism, until then unknown in the Bohemian city marked by the Protestant Hussite culture. Italian Renaissance architecture also appeared, with the most beautiful example being the Belvedere Palace near the castle, which Ferdinand built for his wife Anna. In 1547, however, the policy of affirming royal power provoked a revolt by the nobility and city, harshly repressed with the restriction of the powers they had

36-37 top The 1585 parchment in the picture, with a wealth of detail and refined ornamentation, inspired by Pompeian grotesques, illustrates scenes of life at the court of Prague: the imperial banquet and the awarding of the Golden Fleece.

37 center This portrait of the Emperor Rudolph II, the work of Hans von Aachen, reveals the rather unhappy appearance of the controversial sovereign: apparently arrogant and taciturn, he was capable of generosity and tolerance.

37 bottom A great collector and lover of art, Rudolph II favored the Milanese Guiseppe Arcimboldo, who portrayed him in 1591, two years before his death, in an unusual way, in the guise of Vertumnus, the god of seasons.

gained thanks to the Hussite revolution. From the point of view of religion too, Rome tried increasingly to re-establish its influence and, in 1565, despatched the first Jesuits to Prague. To counter its University, impregnated with Utraquistism, they founded the Klementinum college. The successor to Ferdinand I, his son Maximillian II (1564-1576), whilst being an Hapsburg, was close to the Lutherian confession and would have liked to restore religious liberty to the oppressed Bohemians but was unable to complete his projects. With Rudolf II (1576-1611), a new epoch began for Prague. First and foremost the young emperor preferred the city as his residence to Vienna and there followed paternal teachings attempting to heal the conflicts between the various factions. Described as a mad king because towards the end of his reign he became mentally unstable, in reality Rudolf was a complex and appealing figure. A passionate lover of art, he amassed a precious collection. His court was frequented by the likes of the painter Giuseppe Arcimboldo and the astronomers Tycho Brahe of Denmark and Johannes Kepler.

The country in the meantime experienced profound political and religious upheaval and, in 1609, the emperor, encouraged by the pressure from his younger brother Matthias, issued the *Majestat*, the Letter of Majesty, guaranteeing religious freedom. In spite of this, in 1611 he was obliged to cede the Bohemian throne to Matthias (1611-1619). Matthias was in turn succeeded by Ferdinand II (1619-1637), under whose reign occurred the second "Defenestration of Prague," considered to be the start of the Thirty Years War. This time the emperor's two advisors were thrown from a window in the castle on the 23rd of May, 1618, as a protest by the Bohemian representatives against the religious restrictions and the king's absolutism.

1. Unser Frawen.
2. S. Thomas.
3 S. Nicolas.
4. S. Wensel.
5. S. Martin.
6. Altstatt.
7. Iesuuiter kirchen.
8. Bruck thurn.
9. Grob geschutz.
10. Rathauß so gesturmpt.
11. Saxenhaus.
12. Haus so võ den Passawischen angezundet ist.
13. Flasbenck.
14. Kram Laden.

15. Neuser gaß.
16. Obrist Rame.
17. Welsche gaß.
18. Sporer gaß.
19. Gassen nach der schlos stigen.
20. Graff von thurn.
21. Herr von Felß.
22. Herr Wensel Kinski.
23. Scharmutzel der Bemische reuter.
24. Pulfer so von den Passawischen vnuersehns angezunt.
25. Zwey Cornetten Rittmeisters Brendels, so in die Altstatt erschlagen worden.

38 The very Catholic Ferdinand II (1619-1637), Matthias's successor, governed Bohemia in a period of conflict. The most significant events in his reign were the Second Defenestration of Prague, the signal for the start of the Thirty Years War, and the Battle of the White Mountain. On this occasion, 8 November 1620, he defeated Frederick V, the "Winter King," elected by the Bohemian Diet.

EINFAHL DES PASSAW:
ifchen Krigvolcks, in die kleine
Statt Prag. Anno MDC.XI.
den 15. Februarÿ.

38-39 In February 1611, the streets of Prague, and in particular the Old City center, were convulsed by violent tumults. Rudolph II, who had not succeeded in dealing with the religious rift between Catholics and Protestants, was threatened by his brother Matthias, who aspired to the throne. The troops of the Archduke Leopold, perhaps summoned by the King himself, thus entered Prague, but Matthias, arriving at the request of the States, had the better of the situation and forced him to flee. In May the victor received the crown of Bohemia in the Cathedral of Saint Vitus.

39 bottom The Second Defenestration of Prague reflects the rift which took place between the Hapsburgs and the local aristocracy, between Catholics and Protestants, in the Bohemian capital, as in the rest of Europe. In a climate of extreme tension, on 23 May 1618 the Bohemian representatives attacked the chancellery of the Castle and three imperial delegates were thrown out of the window, from a height of 16 meters. They all survived.

39

A year after this episode, the Bohemian Diet chose as king Frederick V, elector Palatine, and on the 8th of November, 1620, the imperial and royal forces clashed at Bilà Hora, or the White Mountain, outside Prague. The defeat of the Bohemian troops was fast. Frederick V, the "Winter King," fled the capital. Emperor Ferdinand's vendetta was savage, with executions in the square of the Old Town and twelve heads of rebels being displayed at the entrance to the Charles Bridge. Rudolf

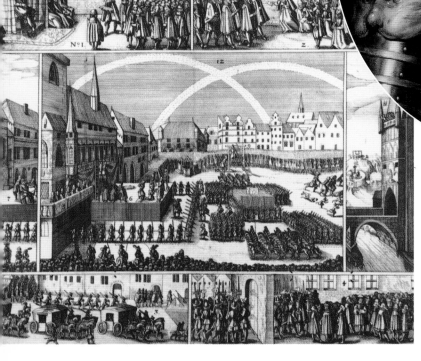

40 top Frederick V, the Elector Palatine Prince, became King of Bohemia on 6 August 1619, after the annulment of the previous election of Frederick II. Greeted with enthusiasm, together with his wife, Elizabeth of England, he disappointed expectations and reigned for a single winter.

40 center The executions of 21 June 1621 on the Old City Square were Ferdinand II's terrible warning to the twenty-seven nobles and citizens for having stirred up the Bohemian revolt against the Hapsburgs. They are recorded by 27 white crosses on the paving of the square.

II's Letter of Majesty was revoked and the Protestant clergy had to leave Prague. The Thirty Years' War rocked the whole of Europe, including Prague. Despite its decadence, in that period the Bohemian city was experiencing the great artistic season of the Baroque style. Along with many churches, the most extravagant palace was built in Malá Strana owned by Albrecht von Wallenstein, a wealthy adventurer and one of the financiers of the war. During the reign of Ferdinand III (1637-1657), the Peace of Westphalia of 1648 put and end to the war; as well as marking the victory of the counter reformation it kept Bohemia and Moravia under Hapsburg domination, giving rise to a period of enforced Catholicism.

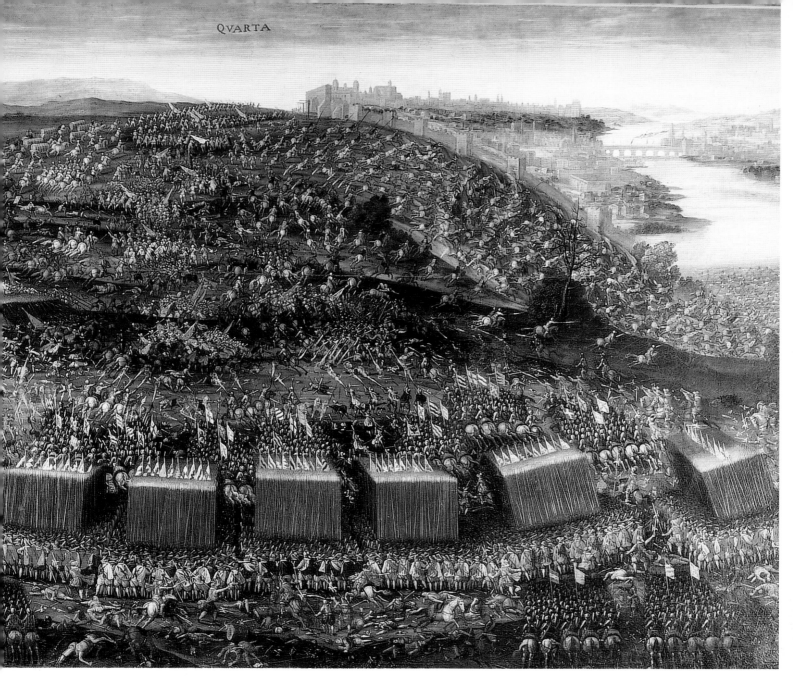

40 bottom The last phase of the Thirty Years War, called the "Franco-Swedish War," began in 1635. When Ferdinand II signed the peace with Prague, Catholic France allied with Protestant Sweden and declared war on the Emperor. In 1638 the Swedes reached Prague and, ten years later, occupied the Castle after bitter fighting on the Charles Bridge, which appears in this painting.

40-41 On 8 November the Battle of the White Mountain, at the gates of Prague, saw the Emperor's army, supported by the Catholic League, ranged against the Bohemian troops of Ferdinand V who,

perhaps not expecting the attack, had remained in the Castle. The battle was decided in a few hours in favor of the imperial troops and the King fled to Holland during the night.

41 bottom The work by Gerard Terboch depicts a fundamental event for 17th-century Europe, disrupted by the Thirty Years' War. On 24 October the Peace of Westphalia was signed which put an end to the conflict, joining the Treaty of Munster between the Emperor and France, and that of Osnabrück between the Emperor and Sweden.

There were a further three Hapsburg kings before the first of the Hapsburg-Lorraine line, Maria Theresa of Austria (1740-1780) and Josef II (1780-1790). Enlightened absolutism characterized these reigns: in 1755, Maria Theresa introduced compulsory education throughout the empire with colleges and secondary schools using Latin and German and the parish schools teaching in the local national languages. In 1781, Josef II issued his Edict of Tolerance which brought an end to the religious wars. The following year he extended the freedom of worship to the Jews. In 1784 the four independent communes of Prague were united in a single administrative body.

On the occasion of the Leopold II's coronation in St. Vitus's Cathedral in 1791, Mozart composed his opera *Titus's Mercy*. From its very outset, the 19th century was characterized by a revival of the Czech national consciousness the focus of which eventually became the National Museum. As early as 1791 Josef Dobrovsky had published a first manifesto regarding the rights of the Czech language that had declined in importance following its elimination by the Bohemian Diet and with the increasing Germanization of the upper classes.

42 Maria Theresa was crowned in the Cathedral of Saint Vitus in a solemn, sumptuous ceremony. The wife of Francis of Lorraine, the Empress' motto was "equity and clemency," and she established compulsory education throughout the kingdom.

42-43 The Empress Maria Theresa, who governed Bohemia with illuminated absolutism from 1740 to 1780, in this canvas by Joseph-Louis Maurice is surrounded by four of her children (she had sixteen): Joseph, her future successor, Ferdinand, Leopold and Maximilian.

43 top The whirl of ladies, *the work of Martin van Meytens dating from the period of the Austrian War of Succession, witnesses a showy, controversial period for Prague:* under the Empress Maria Theresa of Hapsburg, enlightened despotism reached its height, but the Bohemian capital lost rank to the center of the empire, Vienna.

43 bottom The colored drawing by Vincent Morstadt shows an 18th-century view of Prague, with the Charles Bridge in the foreground. The magnificent creation of the architect Peter Parler, one of the symbols of the city, it was the only bridge over the Moldau until 1741.

Czech architects and artists constructed great public buildings such as the National Theater. In the meantime the industrialization of Bohemia, Moravia and Slesia was proceeding apace and the protests of the Czechs, strengthened by the massive urbanization, were increasing. In 1848, the year of the revolutionary storm that swept through Europe, Bohemia included, the Germans and the Czechs, initially united against a common enemy, the Austrian chancellor Metternich, were now divided by an irreparable chasm. Whilst the

Germans were eager to participate in the revolutionary Parliament of Frankfurt, the Czechs wanted a state of their own within the federal Austrian empire. The Slav congress met at Prague on the 2nd of June, 1848, the movement being led by the Czech historian Frantisek Palacky. The population of Prague rose up against the Austrians, but the revolution was suffocated in the blood. The German-speaking Bohemians kept their privileges, and in 1871 the Czech parliament members passed into opposition but a Czech university was reopened.

44 top The Theater of the States General in Prague played a foremost role in the years of nationalist revival. The Czech national anthem, Where my country is, is in fact taken from the musical comedy Fidlovacka, performed there in 1834.

44 bottom In 1848, the year of revolutionary fervor throughout Europe, the Slav Congress met in Prague, demanding equal rights for the various national groups. The divisions, between Germans and Czechs in particular, were then very profound and the Assembly did not achieve significant results. The nationalist revolution, of which this print shows the episode of the barricades, was put down with much bloodshed.

44-45 The Market Square, one of the hubs of Prague life, is seen in this painting dated 1869.

45 top This painting shows the coronation ceremony of Ferdinand I of Austria, who succeeded his father Francis I.

45 bottom This 19th-century watercolor offers a view of the Castle, seen from the nearby hill with its gardens. Amidst the turreted walls, the imposing, but elegant Gothic Cathedral of Saint Vitus stands out.

Following the Sarajevo assassination of 1914, the Czechs unwillingly entered into war and, from the following year the now mature idea of a Czech and Slovak federation was supported by the United States. It can be said that the Republic of Czechoslovakia formed after the armistice of 1918 was the result of the passionate efforts of men such as Tomas Garrigue Masaryk, who became its first president on his return to his homeland after four years of exile, and Edvard Benes, who in 1935 succeeded Masaryk as state president. During the First World War they had managed to open allied eyes to the fundamental role that could be played by a strong Slav block between Germany and Austria. While in 1925 Masaryk had signed a treaty of civil and military alliance with France, Benes, for his part, concluded one with the USSR. The annexation of the new Republic of Sudentenland with its reluctant majority of German-speakers more inclined to an alliance with Austria, some years later provided Hitler with the pretext for attacking Czechoslovakia. In the autumn of 1938, following the Munich Pact, France and Great Britain gave way to Hitler, abandoning Czechoslovakia to its fate in their attempts to maintain peace. Sudentenland, a third of the national territory, passed into the hands of Germany. Benes went into exile in Lon-

don from where he organized the liberal democratic movement. Klement Gottwald, together with other leading figures in the Czech communist party, sought refuge in Moscow.

Following the declaration of the Protectorate of the Third Reich covering Bohemia and Moravia, on the 15th of March, 1939, Hitler's troops occupied Prague. The German-speaking population was satisfied with this change. There began a period of severe repression, the central figure of which was the *Reichsprotektor* Reinhard Heydrich who was subsequently killed by the partisans. Terrible revenge was taken for the killing, with 1,400 people being executed in just two days and the small village of Lidice being completely destroyed.

46-47 *Tomás Garrique Masaryk, the philosopher-president who had organized resistance abroad during the war, and had fought for the birth of the Czech nation, is portrayed as he rides out from the Castle courtyard.*

46 bottom *Edvard Benes, Masaryk's successor at the head of Czechoslovakia in 1937, played an important role in the history of his country, but had to accept the Munich agreements, following which he went into exile to London. He returned as President of the country in 1945.*

47 top *At the Munich conference, held between 19 and 30 September 1938 between the representatives of Germany, Great Britain, France and Italy, the French Premier Edouard Delanier signed the register of those taking part under the watchful eyes of Adolf Hitler. The compromise reached with the Munich Pact was fragile and did not prevent the Führer from invading Czechoslovakia the following year.*

46 top *The declaration of independence of the Czech people, drawn up in his exile in America by T. G. Masaryk and proclaimed in Paris on 18 October 1918, is celebrated in the streets of Prague. Two days before, the change of the monarchy into a Federation of States was voted in Vienna. When Masaryk returned to Prague on 21 December, he was greeted by an enthusiastic crowd.*

The Czechs were by now second class citizens and, according to Hitler, an extraneous body within the German community. When the German Minister of Propaganda, Joseph Goebbels, visited Prague he wrote in his diary, "this is a city that exudes German spirit and it must again be German."

Before the war, fifty percent of all Czech Jews lived in the city, but savage anti-Semitic laws led to the confiscation of goods, generalized repression and to the creation of a transit area for the Polish concentration camps in the fortified city of Terezin, 64 kilometers outside the city. Of the 39,395 Jews deported, no less than 31,709 died. During the war, Prague was spared from aerial bombardment; the first raid was in 1945, when Americans mistook the city for Dresden.

47 center *After the Munich pact, Czechoslovakia was forced to cede the Sudentenland, thus dividing the country. The following year, in March, the Nazi invasion began and Hitler's troops reached Prague.*

47 bottom *It is 1941: the SS General, K.H. Frank and Reichsprotektor Reinhard Heydrich make the Nazi salute in the Castle courtyard. Heydrich was responsible for a ferocious repression.*

48-49 *After coming to power in February 1948, Stalinization became an established fact. An outstanding example of this process and the symbol of the two nations marching towards Communism is the monument to Stalin, overlooking the Moldau. The statue, inaugurated on 1st May 1955, weighed 14,000 tons, was 30 meters high, and was one of the largest in the world. It was knocked down in 1962, during the Kruschev thaw.*

48 top On the morning of 9 May 1945 the first tanks of the Soviet army reached the outskirts of Prague and, joining other divisions coming from Berlin and the Ukraine, overcame the Germans. The population welcomed the liberators and decked their tanks with flowers.

48 center On 15 May 1945 there was a spontaneous uprising against the Germans and Prague was the theater of fierce fighting on the barricades. At the end of the first day of fighting, most of the city east of the river was in the hands of the rebels, and on 8 May they completely controlled the capital. 1694 Czechs lost their lives during the revolt.

48 bottom In February 1948 the Communist coup d'etat took place. The President Edvard Benes, Masaryk's leading disciple, was forced to capitulate in order to avoid civil war. He was replaced a few months later by Clement Gottwald, a loyal supporter of Stalin. His portrait, amidst a riot of red flags, dominates the processions through the streets of the city

49 bottom The Sixties were marked by a serious economic recession, by a certain political thaw and a strong attack on the Soviet-supported system. In 1968 Prague was the scene of lively anti-Communist street demonstrations.

The Prague uprising began on the 5th of May, 1945, and when the Soviet troops arrived four days later they found a liberated city. In the early post-war period, Edvard Benes, back from exile, tried to play off the two blocs that were already facing in Europe; in 1946 the communist Gottwald had formed a coalition government and two years later Benes capitulated in the face of a general strike and the threat of civil war posed by Gottwald, a convinced Stalinist and party leader. He was succeeded by Gottwald himself who committed himself to a brutal process of Sovietization: he nationalized industry, collectivised agriculture and eliminated political adversaries. Labor camps were established and, in 1952, even the general secretary of the party, Rudolf Slànsky, was a victim of a new wave of anti-semitism. The face of Prague itself was also affected, with the construction of the enormous monument to Stalin (among the largest in the world) on the hill of Letnà, subsequently demolished after 1956, and the International Hotel in the Stalinist Gothic style. The Socialist Republic of Czechoslovakia was proclaimed in 1960. The bureaucrat Antonin Novotny, Gottwald's successor, was faced with a serious economic crisis as well as a political thaw and a reawakening of intellectual consciousness that, in 1968, led to the events of the "Prague Spring."

50-51 top The terrible pictures of the Soviet tanks in Prague in August 1968 went around the world. The people of Prague demonstrated and carried out acts of sabotage. The population also attempted to convince the soldiers that the invasion was a serious mistake. In order to prevent problems in the army, the troops were replaced by others from Central Asia.

50-51 bottom This rare photograph documents the burial in the Olsany Cemetery of Jan Palach, who had become the symbol of Czech resistance and the Prague Spring. On 16 January 1969, in Wenceslas Square, the student had set himself on fire. After his death, his funeral turned into an anti-Soviet demonstration.

50 top Alexander Dubcek, a Slovak Communist, took over the party's leadership from the bureaucrat Novotny in 1968. Determined to reform the system, he sought popular support and rejected the authoritarian policies of his predecessor. Under his leadership reforms reached their height: the abolition of censorship, respect for civil rights, the solutions of the Slovak question, the reform of the economy and criticism of the "party's guiding role." Dubcek was also loved by the people because of his modesty and because he embodied "Socialism with a human face."

Incapable of tackling these problems, he had to resign his position as president of the party in favor of the moderate Alexander Dubcek and was replaced as head of state by Ludvìk Svoboda. However, in the August of that year, Soviet tanks entered Prague, shattering the dream of a "socialism with a human face." Around a hundred demonstrators were killed and the following year the student Jan Palach set himself on fire in Wenceslas Square. A totalitarian Stalinist regime was restored in which the Slovak Gustav Usak, first secretary of the party, led the country under the direction of Moscow. In the years of the so-called "normalization" the Czechoslovakian Communist party expelled 500,000 of its members. The Czech borders were closed in October 1969.

51 top The Communist Gustav Husák had taken part in the Anti-German resistance and became head of the provisional government in 1945. Dismissed during the 1951 Stalinist purges of Novotny, after being re-established, he supported Dubcek's new policy, to then distance himself from it after the Soviet invasion, Husák was Party Secretary from 1968 and President of the Czech Republic from 1975 to 1989.

51 bottom During the 1948 coup, General Ludvík Svoboda had guaranteed Gottwald with the army's support, but he was removed from office by non-Communist elements. Dismissed from power in the early Fifties, he was elected President in 1968 and then re-elected in 1973.

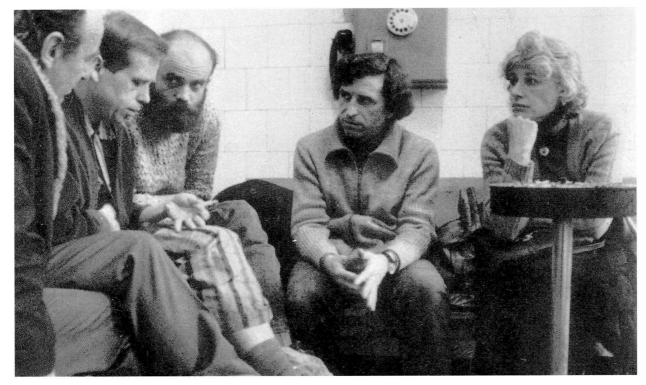

*52 top In February
1983, Václav Havel,
imprisoned for over
four years, was released
for health reasons, and
hospitalized. In the
photograph he appears
with his wife Olga, his
great supporter in
those difficult years,
and his brother Ivan,
together with other
members of the
Charter 77 dissident
movement.*

*52-53 In memory of
Jan Palach, the people
of Prague improvised
night watches and
imposing, peaceful
demonstration during
the so-called "Velvet
Revolution" in 1989.*

The opposition had not been completely extinguished, however, and in 1977 Prague saw the birth of a civil rights movement based on a document (*Charter 77*), being signed by over 200 intellectuals, including the playwright and poet Václav Havel. His ideas and activities in favor of democracy led to him being banned from the theatrical world and he was imprisoned on a number of occasions. Even though *perestrojka* became official policy in 1986, the Velvet Revolution broke out in 1989 with popular demonstrations, marches and political negotiations; Husák resigned and, on the 29th of December, Havel was elected as president of Czechoslovakia. Alexander Dubcek, the key figure in the Prague Spring, was elected speaker of parliament. In 1990, in the first democratic elections to be held for almost sixty years, Havel's Civic Forum got 60% of the votes cast and he was reconfirmed as President. Since the 1st of January, 1993, following the separation from Slovakia (now an independent republic), Prague has been the capital of the Czech Republic which has over 10 million inhabitants. In January, 1993, Havel was elected as the first President of the Czech state.

*53 top A group of
students in Wenceslas
Square wearing gas
masks to express their
feelings concerning
the new government,
dominated by
Communists. In the
demonstration of 4
December 1989 a
demonstration of
about 250,000 people
was held in the city
square.*

*53 bottom On 29
December 1989 the
playwright and
writer Václav Havel,
elected President of
Czechoslovakia,
makes the victory sign
to the citizens
gathered to welcome
him below the Castle.
Hável, a dissident
and one of the writers
of Charter 77, had
been arrested several
times and had
animated the years
before the Velvet
Revolution.*

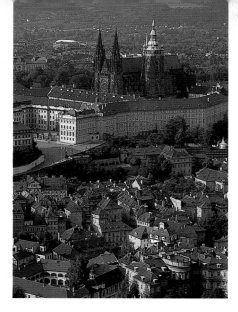

THE LEFT BANK, FROM THE CASTLE TO THE CHARLES BRIDGE, FROM GOTHIC TO BAROQUE

54-55 In one of the most photographed views of the Old City we see the Moldau, the Castle and the Charles Bridge, a favorite Prague walk with tourists who, apart from admiring the statues and the view, stop to purchase craft products and views of the city, sold by the artists themselves.

54 top Illumination transforms the atmosphere of Prague by night and the gate of the Castle entrance, in Hradcanské Námesti takes on even more spectacular connotations. Behind the buildings of the west wing, on which the elegant Matthias Gate opens, may be glimpsed the slender towers of the Cathedral of Saint Vitus.

55 top The Castle buildings, seen from the hill above near the Strahov Monastery, are seen in all the grandiosity and variety of their architecture.

Beginning a visit to Prague with the castle is like leafing through a history book, sampling all the different architectural styles found in the city. But it also means finding oneself where spiritual and temporal powers have always had their site and where still today the President of the Republic has his official residence. The very entrance to the great complex, surrounded by curtain walls enclosing palaces and monasteries, churches and gardens, announces the majesty of what we are about to see.

Only an aerial view, or one from the banks of the River Vltava, can reveal the might and beauty of the castle. It is composed of a series of buildings including the unmistakeable Gothic silhouette of St. Vitus's Cathedral with its flying buttresses, ogival windows, and pinnacles like flame tongues. For over a thousand years, with few interruptions, the destiny of the country has been decided within the walls of the castle, the foundation of which dates back to Borivoj, the first prince of the Premyslid dynasty. On a pagan religious site he ordered the costruction of a wooden fortress and a church, emblem of the ongoing Christianization. The Premyslids adopted the complex as their residence and, from 973, it also became a bishophric. Each sovereign and each historical period had its effect on the castle's appearance featuring various architectural styles from Romanesque to Gothic, Renaissance and Baroque. The result is a kind of citadel, accessed by a number of roads, such as the majestic Hradcanske námestí.

57 The giant statues above the first Castle gate are copies of the originals by the sculptor Ignaz Platzer the Elder and date back to 1768.

Those on the pillars are also by him, and represent the symbols of the Czech kingdom and the Hapsburg monarchy: the lion and the eagle.

A wrought-iron gateway, flanked by the powerful 18th-century *Battling Titans* by Ignaz Platzer, leads into the first courtyard laid out in the Theresian era and dominated by the Matthias Gate (Matyásova brána) from 1614, the first example of Baroque architecture in the whole of the castle. To its right, a Rococo staircase leads to the presidential apartments. The second courtyard, revised during the era of the Hapsburg empress, retains traces of the Romanesque fortifications. The most important building is, on the south side, the Chapel of the True Cross, designed by the Italian Nicolò Pacassi in the late-Baroque style like the sandstone fountain decorated with sculptures of divinities by Hieronymous Kohl. On the north side of the courtyard, the old stables now house the castle gallery. Unfortunately the extraordinary collection amassed by Rudolf II has, over the centuries and after many wars, been dispersed throughout Europe, but around seventy fine works remain including paintings by Titian, Tintoretto, Veronese and Rubens.

56 top left The Castle entrance is guarded, apart from the giants, by soldiers in uniform whose changing of the guard is highly popular with visitors. In the background, in the first courtyard stands out the Matthias Gate in sandstone, a fine example of the first Prague Baroque period, the work of Nicolò Pacassi.

56 bottom left In the second courtyard, the Baroque fountain is the work of Francesco de Torre and the sculptor Jaromír Kohl. In the central part, the statues of Hercules and Neptune, Vulcan and Mercury support a platform with three tritons who, in turn, support the upper part, decorated with three lions.

56 top right The Holy Cross Chapel, in the second courtyard of the Castle, was built to the design of Nicolò Pacassi in the second half of the 18th century, to replace that of Saint Wenceslas. Of the inside only the main altar with sculptures of angels by I. F. Platzer remain.

56 bottom right The decoration of the Holy Cross Chapel dates back to the restoration work of 1852-56, when it became the private chapel of the Emperor Ferdinand V the Good. The ceiling frescoes depict Old Testament scenes, while those on the walls show episodes from the New Testament.

58 top left In the third courtyard of the Castle stands the copy of the famous statue of Saint George, now kept in the National Gallery, cast in 1375 by Jíri and Martin of Kluz. It is the oldest example of non-decorative Gothic work in Bohemia: it was in fact designed to be displayed alone and not within another context.

59 top left The central portal of the Cathedral, a detail of whose dedication is seen in the picture, documents scenes relating to its construction and portrays the architects and artists who worked on it.

59 bottom left This marble slab by the door illustrates, above, the episode in which Saint Wenceslas receives the relics of Saint Vitus from the Emperor's hands, and also the foundation of the Rotunda of Saint Vitus and its dedication.

59 top right In this fine picture of the cathedral seen from the back, the Gothic buttress system stands out, recalling the "City of God" which the sacred building represented. From this view Saint Vitus truly looks like a thick wood of stone.

59 bottom right The lower part of the western facade of Saint Vitus appears like stone lace-work. The front in sandstone is decorated by 20th-century bas reliefs, depicting the Nativity, the Crucifixion and the Assumption of Christ; the imposing rose window with its 10.40 meter diameter fits into a pointed window.

58 bottom left The Gothic gargoyles, under the roof adorned with spires, which collect rain water, are in the guise of devils and monstrous figures to protect the Cathedral from evil influences or, according to another version, to invite the worshippers to leave impure, sinful thoughts outside its walls.

58 right The magnificent large rose window in the west facade of the Cathedral is a modern work of 1921 by Frantysek Kysela: it represents scenes from Genesis and, at the sides, portraits of the Cathedral architects.

One gains the greatest impression on entering the third and oldest courtyard, dominated by the soaring spires of St. Vitus's Cathedral. Work on this magnificent building, which harmoniously combines various architectural styles from Gothic to Baroque and Art Nouveau, continued for five centuries. It was begun in 1344 on the site of the Romanesque rotunda of the same name and often interrupted by the Hussite wars and lack of funds, only being completed in 1929. The west facade in the Neo-Gothic style dates, in fact, from this last period and features a rose window 10 meters in diameter flanked by portraits of the last architects. The towers are embellished with fourteen statues of saints. On the three contemporary bronze doors can be read, in the center the complex history of the cathedral, on the left the life of St. Wenceslas and on the right that of St. Adalbert. The south side, which for many centuries was the principal facade, is dominated by the Golden Door, named after the luminous mosaic of the *Last Judgement* in the Venetian style (14th century), through which the kings entered for their coronation ceremonies. The light Gothic arches of the door, supported by a complex bundle of ribs are one of the masterpieces of Peter Parler. The slim Renaissance tower has a roof in the Baroque style. Before entering the cathedral one cannot but admire the audacity, lightness and decorations of the flying buttresses that surround the nave and the choir.

This last element, again by Peter Parler (1385), boasts a remarkable interior with audacious ogival vaults as well as an impressive dais and a triforium with a gallery of Gothic sculptures, the busts of the 21 founders and patrons of the church. The stained-glass windows in some of the chapels by famous Czech artists of the 20th century such as Max Svabinsky (first right) and Alfons Mucha (third left), successfully introduce Prague Art Nouveau into the Gothic setting. The cathedral's 21 side chapels (the plan of the building features three naves with a transept and ambulatory) provide a veritable tour through Bohemian art and history. The cathedral interior is bathed in

the unique light filtered by the stained-glass windows in the choir and the side chapels as well as the great rose window with its 27,000 fragments of multi-colored glass. The chromatic effects have symbolic meanings. The sacred space of the temple, a kind of celestial Jerusalem removed from the world, should in fact be illuminated not by the natural light of the heavenly bodies, but by the more mysterious and mystical glory of God. There is, however, another interpretation of the not solely aesthetic significance of the stained-glass windows in that they provide a precious separation of the earthly experience from the divine reality of which only glimpses are possible during life.

61 left The glass window of the New Bishop's Chapel in the Cathedral was built to a design by the great Czech painter Alfons Mucha, an illustrious representative of the Secession style. Inspired by Slav folklore, the work shows scenes from the lives of Saints Cyril and Methodius.

61 right The glass window of the Schwarzenberg Chapel, designed by Karel Svolinsky, depicts scenes from the life of Adam Frantisek Schwarzenberg and the story of the relics of Saint John Nepomuceno.

61

The most famous and extraordinary of the cathedral's chapels, the work of Parler (1362-64) and dedicated to St. Wenceslas, the patron saint of Bohemia, glitters with semi-precious stone (amethysts, jasper, chalcedony) and gold-leaf. The life of the saint is depicted, along with the passion of Christ, in the 16th-century frescoes on its walls, while the Gothic statue (1372) is by Heinrich Parler, grandson of the architect. Another of the chapels, the tomb of St. John of Nepomuceno, is even more sumptuous thanks to the use of over two tonnes of silver. It was created between 1733 and 1736 by Antonio Corradini and the Viennese goldsmith Jan Josef Wurth. The story of Nepomuceno, martyred in 1393 and proclaimed a saint in 1729, is unusual. Due to the people's veneration of Jan Hus, the Church searched for another martyr, the Jesuits eventually coming up with their vicar general John of Pomuk, Nepomuceno. As the legend goes he had been thrown into a sack and drowned in the Vltava under the Charles Bridge for not having revealed to King Wenceslas IV the confessional secrets of his wife Sophia.

In the royal crypt, which is accessed from the chapel of the True Cross, lie Charles IV, his children, his four wives, Wenceslas IV, Ladislao Postumo, George of Prodebrady, Rudolf II and Maria Amalia, daughter of the empress Maria Theresa, all in sarcophagi from the 1930s. Below the crypt, directly in front of the Neo-Gothic High Altar, stands the white marble 16th-century royal mausoleum of the Hapsburgs by the Dutchman Alexander Collin. The mausoleum is closed by a magnificent Renaissance gateway. Behind the High Altar there are also the tombs of the Premyslid princes and, on the south side, the Royal or Vladislav Jagiellonian Oratory, an extraordinary example of naturalistic Gothic with intertwining branches created by Benedikt Ried in 1493. A corridor links the oratory to the building that from the 9th to the 16th century was the royal palace until the Habsburgs preferred the new wing of the castle. The various phases of the cathedral's construction can be read as if in an open book on the north facade: the arches date from the first 13th-century residence of Otokar II, the buttresses are late-Gothic while the windows are Renaissance in style.

62 top left The silver tomb of Saint John Nepomuceno is the largest work in precious metal in Bohemia. It was constructed between 1733 and 1736 by the goldsmith J.J. Würth to a design by J. B. Fischer of Erlach. Above the funerary monument hangs a canopy, the gift of the Empress Maria Theresa.

62 top right The late-Gothic royal oratory takes up the upper part of the vestibule and was commissioned by Vladislav Jagiellon in 1493. It is probably the work of Hans Spiess and Benedikt Ried. The fine plant-design ornamentation bears the royal monogram sculpted on the hanging key; the coats of arms are those of the countries ruled by Jagiellon.

62 bottom right The royal mausoleum of the Hapsburgs is under the crypt containing the bronze and tin coffins of Charles IV, Wencelas IV, George of Podebrad and Rudolph II.

62-63 The Saint Wencelas Chapel, with the relics of the country's patron saint, is the most precious and sacred in the Cathedral. It is larger than the other chapels and has a magnificent star-shaped vault and walls covered in a mosaic of 1,345 pieces in precious stones.

63 bottom The wooden bas relief of 1620, The Flight of Frederick II from Prague (which took place after his defeat at the Battle of the White Mountain), is composed of two panels, situated in the ambulatory, between the arches of the choir of Saint Vitus's. It gives a faithful view of the city of Prague around 1635. The statue in the background is that of Cardinal Schwarzenberg.

The Vladislav Hall is reached by way of the Green Room, the setting for Charles IV's law court and for royal hearings during the reign of Ferdinand I. The imposing hall (62 meters long, 13 high and 16 broad), embellished with complex rib vaults, was created by Benedikt Ried between 1493 and 1503, and represents a remarkable example of late-Gothic architecture; its large windows are, however, a prelude to the Renaissance. Standing under the sublime vaults it is not difficult to evoke the banquets and tournaments that were held here. To reach the hall the knights on chargers climbed the magnificent Knights' Staircase with its ribbed vaults and broad steps.

Another staircase, at the back of the Vladislav Hall leads to the All Saints Chapel, a private church belonging to the noble convent and, following a fire, rebuilt in the Italian Renaissance style. The Diet Hall, also by Ried but remodelled in 1500, is an historic room which held the meetings of the Diet, hence the throne, the archbishop's chair on its right and the tribune for the judges and the representatives of the royal cities. On the walls are portraits of the Hapsburg emperors.

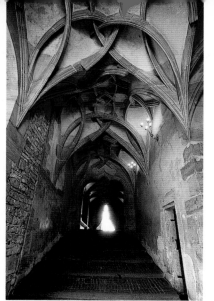

Leaving the palace by way of the Knights' Staircase, one finds oneself in the small, suggestive St. George's Square (Jirské Námestí), dominated by the Baroque facade of the basilica. In reality this is one of the oldest Romanesque monuments in Bohemia, as testified by the two lateral towers. St. George's was built during the reign of Vratislav I, and in 924 Saint Ludmilla, the grandmother of St. Wenceslas, was buried here. The foundations of the adjacent Benedictine convent, the first in Bohemia, date from 973, the era of Boleslav II, the building being erected at the behest of his sister Mlada. In spite of the various revisions, the basilica has a severe atmosphere evocative of the second half of the 12th century. It has three naves, a raised rectangular choir and three semi-circular apses.

In the Gothic chapel of Saint Ludmilla, to the right of the choir, stands her 14th-century tomb (from the workshop of Peter Parler): in front of it rest Vratislav I and Boleslav II. The abbesses of the convent, including Mlada, are buried in the crypt.

The monastery of St. George today houses the National Gallery's beautiful collection of ancient Bohemian art featuring a precious group of Gothic madonnas. Among the fortifications behind the convent built on the orders of Vladislav Jagiellon, the 15th-century Dalibor Tower is associated with one of the various Prague legends, that of the young knight imprisoned there while awaiting execution. He played the violin so well that the people brought him food and appealed in vain for his liberation. The composer Smetana immortalized this melancholic figure in his romantic work *Dalibor*.

Between the "Daliborka" and the White Tower winds one of the shortest and most fascinating streets in Prague, the Golden Lane (Zlatá Ulicka). Its colored cottages dating

from 1540 were inhabited that century by a number of master goldsmiths, while the writer Franz Kafka lived at number 22 for a brief period.

All that remains is to discover the more "bucolic" parts of the castle outside the fortifications: the recently restored Royal Gardens, the Tennis pavilion and the Belvedere in pure Renaissance style with its famous singing fountain by the master Jaros.

66-67 A magnificent view of the Castle, with the garden, the Moldau and part of the Old City, showing the Cathedral bell tower, almost 100 meters high.

67 top Six fine sandstone statues by Matyas Bernard Braun, brought from Stirin Castle, today adorn the Hartig Garden which, although historically belonging to the palace of the same name, was annexed to the gardens of Prague Castle in the Sixties.

67 center The Belvedere Garden is framed by the building of the same name, a royal country pavilion, designed by Paolo della Stella in Renaissance style. With its perfect proportions, its hull-shaped roof by the architect Wohlmut, this elegant palace has arches richly decorated with historic and mythological themes.

67 bottom The Tennis Pavilion, a Renaissance building by Bonifaz Wohlmut, is situated in the Royal Garden. Destroyed during the Second World War, it was rebuilt exactly the same, with a facade decorated by allegorical patterns. Its name comes from the game of royal tennis, a sport practiced here by the nobles.

68 top left The photograph shows a detail of the facade of the Archbishop's Palace: the sumptuous porch and the roof-terrace are typically early Gothic, while the rest is Rococo style. The archbishop's coat of arms of Jan Bedrich of Wallenstein stands out in the center.

68 top right The Tuscan Palace, dating back to the late 17th century, was owned by the Duchess Maria Anna of Tuscany until 1918. The Italian coats of arms stand out above the two porches. The upper floor is decorated with statues of ancient divinities, the work of Jan Brokoff.

68-69 On the northern side of Hradcany Square, alongside the Castle, stands the imposing building of the Archbishop's Palace. It was built starting from 1538 in Renaissance style and has since been altered.

69 top In the center of Hradcany Square stands the column of the Virgin Mary, also called "the Plague Column," because it was built in 1715 in gratitude for the end of the epidemic. The fine Baroque statues of the Virgin and Saints surrounding her (also including Saint Charles Borromeo) are the work of Ferdinand Brokoff.

69 center The late-Renaissance facade of Martinic House is decorated with false ashlar work and graffiti, inspired by the Old Testament story of Joseph. It contains precious painted ceilings and frescoes.

69 bottom In Loretánská Street, situated where a path used to lead to the Strakov monastery, stand splendid noble houses, decorated with stuccoes and paintings which often give them their name.

Leaving the castle, one is struck by the harmony of Hradcanské Námestí (to the front) where a series of elegant palaces act as a corona to the 18th-century column commemorating the plague with a statue of Mary by Ferdinand Brokoff.

Alongside the castle is the Archbishop's palace in the Rococo style, dating to the beginning of the second half of the 16th century, which itself stands in front of the High-Baroque Sternberg palace (the work of the architects Martinelli, Dientznehofer and Alliprandi). The National Gallery is housed in its elliptical pavilion. The fine collections of antique European art include masterpieces such as Albrecht Dürer's *Recurrence of Rosario*, Pieter Breugel the Elder's *Haymaking* and Bronzino's *Portrait of Elenor of Toledo*.

The Martinický Palace is striking for its facade decorated with late-Renaissance graffiti depicting *Old Testament* scenes and Greek mythology. In front of the Martinický rises the magnificent Schwarzenberský palace created by Agostino Galli in 1545-63 in the Czech Renaissance style (high, pointed gables, facades with painted graffiti decoration and ashlar work). A last grand building closes the square to the west, the 17th-century Toscana palace, so-named because it belonged to the dukes of Tuscany. It boasts an extremely attractive facade featuring two belvederes with statues.

70-71 One of the most illustrious masterpieces in the National Gallery of Art is without a doubt the magnificent *Feast of the Rose Garlands*, *by Albrecht Dürer (1506). The altar-piece was originally housed in the Church of Saint Bartholomew in Venice and was acquired by Rudolph II for his extraordinary collection.*

71 top *The refined* Portrait of Eleonora of Toledo, *the daughter of the Viceroy of Naples, is by Angelo Allori, called "Il Bronzino." The mannerist painter focused his attention on the preciousness of her red gown, with its gold embroidery, and on the noblewoman's right hand, adorned with two showy rings.*

71 center left *This is one of the most famous of Rembrandt's paintings. Entitled* The Scholar, *it was completed in 1634.*

71 center right *This portrait of Ambrogio Spinola, the work of Peter Paul Rubens, is dated 1627, three years before the death of the Ligurian nobleman. Spinola commissioned the work before the disastrous Casale campaign, which was fatal for his military career in Spanish pay.*

71 bottom *Peter Breughel the Elder's bucolic compositions with its celebrated series of Months, number among the masterpieces in the National Gallery. Breughel's paintings are found in the large section dedicated to Flemish painting: thanks to a donation, the Gallery possesses an important collection of works from the Netherlands.*

72 top left On the upper floor of the convent is found the Theological Room, originally a library, created by the Italian Orsi from 1671-79. The pictures illustrate

literary themes. The engraved bookcases are of great value. In Baroque style, they contain some 16,000 works, including the Kralice Bible and precious incunabula.

73 top right The Loreto Sanctuary, the work of Giovanni Battista Orsi, was built in 1626-27 at the wish of the noblewoman Katerina of Lobkovice. Every hour the 18th century bell rings in the bell tower, the work of Kilian Ignaz Dientzenhofer, as is the Church of the Nativity and the main front.

73 bottom right In the Sanctuary courtyard is situated the Holy House, a copy of the house of the Virgin Mary at Nazareth. According to the legend, in the late 14th century, when the Muslims occupied the Holy Places, the angels brought it to safety in Loreto, Italy. The Holy House has always been venerated and in the Baroque period copies rose throughout Europe.

72 top right Schwarzenberg House, a 16th century work by Alfonso Galli, echoes Florentine Renaissance in its refined facade, on which skillful graffiti create an ashlar effect. It houses the Museum of Military History.

72-73 The Premonstratensi Monastery in Strahov, in the Castle district, was founded by Vladislav II. The original foundations of the convent and abbey church, which were later rebuilt in Baroque style, have been preserved until the present day. The monastery was always an important cultural center in the country, and the 18th century Philosophical Room, the work of Ignazio Palliardi, has a ceiling frescoed with the theme of the history of mankind in search of true wisdom.

73 left The present-day appearance of the Church of the Assumption, in the Strahov Monastery, is dated 1758. Inside, the vaults are decorated with frescoes by Josef Kramolin, while the side lunettes are the work of the brush of Ignaz Raab. In Saint Ursula's Chapel, beneath the altar, lies Saint Norbert's body.

Loretánská leads to Loretánská Námestí with the monumental Cernínsky Palace (1699-79), the work of Francesco Caratti and Anselmo Lurago who designed the portal almost a century later. The square is dominated and takes its name, however, from the Prague Loreta shrine (the most famous in Bohemia), built at the behest of a noblewoman in order to spread the cult of the Holy House of the Virgin. The shrine also fell within the ambit of the promotion of the Catholic faith warmly advocated by Ferdinand II after the victory of the White Mountain. The whole grandiose complex rose around the Holy House, a chapel decorated with Italian relief sculptures and stucco-work. The Baroque Church of the Nativity, one of Prague's most elegant, has Rococo frescoes and paintings. The facade dating from 1721 is divided into two lateral wings and a central body topped by an onion dome from where a peal of bells sounds a melody by Dvorák based on the theme of a traditional Bohemian song.

On a hill a short distance away, but on the confines of the Malá Strana quarter, rises another of the great Prague institutions, the Premonstratensian Strahovsky. Founded in 1140 by the monks of the order of St. Norbert, destroyed by a fire and rebuilt in the Baroque style, Strahovsk´y was always a seat of learning thanks to its famous library which boasts a celebrated 9th-centu-

ry evangelary. The library's Theological Hall, a spectacular example of Baroque decoration, contains maps of the world, books, rare manuscripts and the *Vysehrad Codex*. The Philosophical Hall, with its over 50,000 volumes is famed for its magnificent ceiling frescoed by the Rococo painter Franz Maulbertsch with allegorical scenes. The Baroque church of Our Lady of the Assumption, decorated with scenes from the life of St. Norbert, contains an organ played by Mozart.

The Malá Strana (little city) quarter that from the mid-13th century has occupied the slopes of the castle hill, is the Baroque "jewel" of Prague. Nothing has been built here since 1700 and its magnificent palaces, churches and squares form a complex of rare harmony and beauty. Its position gives the quarter the appearance of being in the lap of the castle but, as has already been mentioned, this self-contained area of Prague neither looks towards the imposing bulk of the citadel nor the waters of the Vltava. In reality Malá Strana, founded by Otokar II Premsyl in 1257, was profoundly marked by the building program of Charles IV and enjoys something of an autonomous existence. Its architecture is a magnificent jumble of towers and mansard roofs, chimney pots and roof-terraces, stucco and paintings, that overlook doorways decorated with arabesques. Its alleyways, its narrow, winding streets have at times a mysterious air and lead to secret corners or stop before ancient walls from which sprout the tops of trees and behind which one may guess the presence of tranquil gardens. One has to imagine Malá Strana in the centuries gone by when, with its rich palaces and sumptuous churches, it acted as the backdrop to the last stretch of the "coronation route." On Malostranské námestí (the Little Side Square), the elegant, colorful procession would pause before tackling the last section up to the castle, the precipitous street now called Nerudova.

It would be accompanied by the joyful sound of the bells that still today ring out from the numerous bell-towers. The focal point of the quarter is in fact Malostranské Námestí around the Baroque church of St. Nicholas, the tapering tower of which, by Anselmo Lurago, and the great gold dome, 75 meters high, are the dominant vertical features in the area. Built between 1704 and 1755 by the great architects Dientzenhofer, father and son, and Lurago, this church was intended to demonstrate the power of the Jesuits. The interior is richly decorated with pictorial and sculptural works of art, including a magnificent pulpit with gilded cherubs and the grandiose fresco of the central nave, one of the largest in Europe, with scenes of the life of St. Nicholas. This fresco was executed by J. L. Kracker whilst the one in the dome, *The Holy Trinity in Glory* is the work of F. X. Palko. Mozart played the great Baroque organ in 1787 and, shortly after his death, over 4,000 people gathered in the church for the requiem mass in his honor. Among the square's other beautiful buildings is the Renaissance house on Gothic foundations, the "House of the Golden Lion," which is now the home of the famous restaurant "U Mecenáse." The upper part of Malostranské Námestí is instead occupied by the large Lichtenstejnský Palace with its neo-classical facade. At one time this was the home of the "Bloody Governor" who sent to their deaths the leaders of the opposition to Ferdinand II. It now houses the Academy of Music.

Climbing towards the castle from Malostranské Námestí along the last section of the "coronation route," Nerudova is one of Prague's most beautiful streets. It takes its name from Jan Neruda, the author of the *Stories of Malá Strana,* who lived in the "House of the Two Suns" (No. 47) between 1845 and 1857. It is not perhaps widely known that the Chilean poet Pablo Neruda adopted his surname in his honor.

Only in 1770 were house numbers introduced to Prague, and this street features a fascinating collection of signs and coats of arms that were previously used to distinguish the individual buildings. Among the most interesting buildings is the Renaissance-style "House of the Three Violins" (No. 12) of the Edlinger violin makers and that of "The Gold Cup" (No. 16). At No. 18 is the "House of St. John Nepomuceno," with the symbol of the saint and the remains of graffiti decoration. Many of these buildings house evocative cafés and bars that are very popular with the citizens of Prague. The Thun-Hohenstejnský Palace (No. 20), the home of the Italian embassy, is one of the most beautiful Baroque buildings in Bohemia, as is the Morozinský Palace (No. 95), the Romanian embassy building, with its imposing sculptural decoration. Returning to Malastranské Námestí, on the corner between the extremely lively Letenská and Tommaská, is the historic Schnell beer cellar, the favorite of the Russian Czar Peter the Great.

80-81 Waldstein (Wallenstein) House, which belonged to Albrecht of Wallenstein, the famous imperial army General, is one of the largest, most sumptuous Baroque buildings in Prague. The work of the architects Pieroni, Spezza and Segrebondi, it dates back to the period of the Thirty Years War, between 1623 and 1630.

80 bottom left The Holy Trinity Column, in the upper part of Malastraneské Námesti, is also called "the Plague Column." It was in fact erected in 1715 to mark the end of the epidemic. The votive monument, decorated with statues of the Trinity, Virgin Mary and five patron saints of Bohemia, is the work of G.B. Aliprandi.

80 bottom right Every facade in Malá Strana holds a surprise in store, like a successful stage setting, which changes scenery between the acts. Renaissance motifs and frescoes intermingle with Baroque. The contrasts of color and decoration on plant and heraldic animal themes achieve notable plastic effects.

A short distance away stand the church and monastery of St. Thomas (with Prague's oldest beer cellar) founded in the late 13th century by the Agostinian order and later rebuilt in the Baroque style by Kilian Ignaz Dientzenhofer. In this area, in which a number of embassies and ministries are located, there are also many magnificent palaces and gardens. Valdstejnské Námestí, one of the most romantic squares in Prague, is dominated by the palace of the same name (also known as the Wallenstein), the city's grandiose, first secular building in the Baroque style. A fresco on the ceiling of the Great Hall depicts the ambitious imperial general, Wallenstein, as Mars. The park, accessed from Letenská, is enchanting, with its fountains, bronze statues, a pavilion frescoed with the legend of the Argonaut's search for the Golden Fleece and a grotto. Another of Malá Strana's singular and attractive squares is Maltezské Námestí (the Maltese Square), with a sculptural group portraying St. John the Baptist, the Maltese patron saint, by F. Brokoff. Maltezké Námestí is reached from Malostranské Námestí by way of Mostecká (Bridge Street) and Lásenská, famous for its beautiful, aristocratic houses. There are two old hostelries at No. 6 and No. 11, the "House of the Bath" and the "House of the Golden Unicorn" where, as plaques state, Peter the Great and Chateaubriand, Mozart and Beethoven stayed. The Church of Mary in Chains, the church of the Knights of Malta, is the oldest in the quarter (12th century) and boasts a magnificent baroque interior.

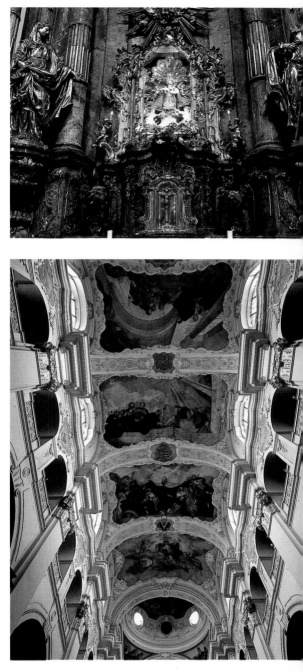

81 top A refined marble altar in the right nave of Saint Mary of Victory holds the venerated wax statue of the Child Jesus of Prague, brought from Spain at the end of the 16th century, and donated to the Carmelites in 1628 by a noblewoman. According to the religious service, the precious clothes on the statue are changed: they were the gift of famous people, such as the Empress Maria Theresa of Austria.

81 center The theatrical central Baroque nave of the Church of Saint Thomas glows with the frescoes by V.V. Reiner, illustrating the life of Saint Augustine. He also painted the frescoes in the dome and the presbytery.

81 bottom Lazenská Street is overlooked by fine noble aristocratic houses and inns, such as "the Baths" (where the Russian Tzar Peter the Great and the writer René Chateaubriand stayed) and "The Golden Unicorn" where a young Beethoven stayed in 1796.

Not far away, on Karmelitská, is one of the most venerated churches, St. Mary of the Victory. Originally a German Lutheran church, it was converted by the Spanish Discalced Carmelites and thus named in honor of the Catholic victory at the White Mountain. The city's first baroque church, it houses the wax statuette of the Baby Jesus of Prague, held to be miraculous since the 17th century. Even the empress Maria Theresa was devoted to the icon and donated many gold brocade robes to it. Returning to Maltézké Námestí, once characterized by the Renaissance-style residences of the wealthy bourgeoise, what are striking today are the Baroque and Rococo buildings that belonged to the Catholic nobility. The Turba and Nostitz Palaces are respectively the Japanese and Dutch embassies. Even more extravagant is the 18th-century Palace of the Grand Master of the Order of Malta, on the square of the same name, that today houses a museum of musical instruments. Its beautiful gardens are frequently used to stage summer concerts. A bridge crossing the Devil's Stream (Certovká), a branch of the Vldava, here links Malá Strana with the island of Kampa. The stream once served to power the mills of which three can still be seen. The whole of Malá Strana has a tranquil atmosphere with almost timeless corners, but on the island one breathes a truly intimate and provincial air. Kampa boasts an attractive and luxuriant park composed of various gardens, a central square, Na Kampè, with lampposts and beautiful Renaissance and Baroque houses, and an evocative area known as the "Venice of Prague."

84 top The 19th-century copy of the statue of the knight Bruncvík stands on a pillar of the Charles Bridge.

84 center One of the finest groups of sculptures on the Charles Bridge is that of the Dream of Saint Lutgarda, *the work of Matthias Braun.*

84 bottom The Charles Bridge is a veritable open-air sculpture gallery: there are 32 statues and groups of sculptures of great value.

A flight of steps leads to the Charles Bridge, the architectural marvel started in 1357 by Peter Parler but only completed at the beginning of the 15th century. The appeal of the bridge derives from the contrast between the severe Gothic architecture and the Baroque opulence of the statues. For the latter the model was undoubtedly the Sant'Angelo Bridge in Rome. The sculptural decoration consisting of 26 statues and groups was created by the most celebrated artists, between 1706 and 1714. A further two were added in 1857 and 1859 while the most recent works portray-ing the evangelist saints Cyril and Methodius instead date from 1938. Over the centuries the statues have been subject to replacement and rotation due to various motives, some of them political. Today many of the original sculptures are to be found in the National Museum. For two hundred years a wooden crucifix was the bridge's only decoration but this was eliminated during the era of the Hussite wars. The current bronze crucifix came from Dresden and dates back to the 17th century. The first saint to appear on the bridge was John Nepomuceno sculpted in 1683 by M. Rach-

84-85 *The Charles Bridge, seen here in the stretch looking towards Malá Strana, dates back to 1300. Two towers stand out in the background: the lower is Romanesque, while the higher one was erected in 1464 on the model of that on the opposite bank, the work of Peter Parler. In the foreground is the statue of Saint Adalbert, the Bishop of Prague.*

85 left *This view bears witness to the love of the people of Prague and tourists for the Charles Bridge, as they cross it on their daily walk.*

(Brokoff, 1714) who, dressed as a Roman legionnaire, is perched on a rock, watched by predatory lions. On one of the bridge's piers standing on the island of Kampa, rises the 16th-century statue of the knight Brunevik that was intended to celebrate the victory of the bourgeoisie over the nobles regarding the payment of rights.

A humorous legend surrounds the construction of the bridge; it appears that in order to make the cement stronger by adding egg yolks, consignments of this unusual and rather fragile "material" arrived from all over the country. The inhabitants of the town of Velvary, worried that the eggs might break en-route, sent them hard boiled.

muller and J. Brokoff; at the base of the monument the relief sculptures (polished after being touched innumerable times by people seeking good fortune) depict the legend of his death. Of particular pathos and artistic merit is the sculptural group of Saint Lutgard (1710) by Mathias B. Braun. Christ revealed himself to the blind Cistercian nun and allowed her to kiss his wounds. Many statues are closely linked to the history of Prague, such as those of Saint Adalbert (Vojtech in Czech), the first Bohemian bishop from the 10th century, Saints Wenceslas and Ludmilla, Saint Vitus

85 top right *The statue of Saint John Nepomuceno is the only one in bronze and the oldest on the Bridge. Prague is full of images of this saint, who was canonized in 1721.*

85 bottom right *A detail of the statue of Saint John Nepomucene shows the parts describing his martyrdom. The surface of the panel is smooth because touching the statue has for centuries been considered to bring good luck.*

86 top left At the end of the Charles Bridge, on the Staré Mesto side, rises the Old City Tower, elegant in its Gothic form. It was built in 1380 by the architect Peter Parler, who designed the Cathedral of Saint Vitus.

86 top right The statue of Charles IV, with the allegorical figures of the four University faculties, was erected in the little Knight of the Cross Square in 1848, to mark the 500th anniversary of the foundation by the Emperor of the University of Prague.

THE RIGHT BANK, FROM THE OLD TOWN TO THE NEW: A WEALTH OF HISTORY

86-87 Alongside the famous Bridge Tower is silhouetted the Water Tower of the Old City, situated in the group of buildings of the little Novotny Bridge.

87 top The picture shows the Moldau with the sunset bathing the Old City in golden light. The towers and domes alternate with facades in a fascinating play of reflections in the placid waters of the river.

87 center The first of the many houses encountered on entering Staré Mesto from the Charles Bridge is the Church of Saint Francis, whose dome majestically overlooks the Bridge.

87 bottom The old library of the Clementinum College was built in 1727 by F. M. Kanka. The ceiling, decorated with allegories of science and art, is by J. Hiebel. The most valuable works include the Vysehrad Code, of 1084.

The magnificent Gothic tower standing on the last pier of the Charles Bridge leads us into the Old Town. The recurrent motif of the ensnared kingfisher was the symbol of Wenceslas IV, the king who had the tower built into the fortified walls of Staré Mesto. It was designed in 1391 by Peter Parler whose workshop was also responsible for the decorative statues on the side facing away from the Vltava: on the upper part stand the patron saints Sigismund and Adalbert while below Saint Vitus is flanked by Charles IV and Wenceslas IV.

A more recent monument to the emperor Charles is also a feature of the facing Krìzovnické Námestí, the small but perfectly formed Knights of the Cross Square. The square's principal building is the Baroque Church of Christ the Savior, one of the three temples of the great Klementium complex, described by one writer as a vast, severe and arrogant bulwark. This former Jesuit college (1653-1723), today the home of the university and national libraries, is the city's largest architectural complex after the castle and was, in fact, built as an affirmation of the power of the Catholic church, distancing the inconvenient ghost of Jan Hus.

The narrow Karlova Ulice, once part of the "coronation route," winds alongside the Klementium and leads to the Old Town square. Always crowded, full of citizens having their traditional city walk, it is today a veritable compendium of souvenir and craft shops.

Among the most beautifully decorated houses overlooking the square are the Baroque "House of the Golden Well" at No. 3, with relief sculptures of saints such as Rocco and Sebastian, believed to provide protection from epidemics; and another in the Secession style featuring Princess Libuse among the roses (No. 22/24).

The Baroque Clam Gallas Palace, the home of the city archive, is the most imposing building on the nearby Husova. Particularly impressive are the two magnificent pairs of muscular Atlantes, the work of Mathis Braun, which replace the columns of the portals and embody an authentic expression of power and beauty. The same sculptor was also responsible for the statues on the great staircase, frescoed by Carlo Carlone in 1730 with the *Triumph of Apollo*.

A side-turning leads to Malé Náměstí (Small Square), a quiet, romantic corner of the city in the center of which is an elegant well with Renaissance ironwork, while at No. 3 is one of Prague's most famous houses, the "House of the Three White Roses," featuring allegorical decorations based on cartoons by Mikolás Ales.

PENZION
RESTAURACE
U ZLATÉ STUDNY

90 top From the Town Hall Tower we have an unusual view of the most famous square in Prague, that of the Old City. The animated play of Romanesque and Gothic houses in pastel shades is like a curious jigsaw puzzle.

90 bottom Stage-like houses, in tender shades, in Romanesque and Gothic style, border the south side of Old City Square. From the right we see "The Golden Unicorn," "U Lazara," restructured in Renaissance style, the Baroque "Stone Table," "The Stone Ram" and "Storch House."

91/94 One of the dominating features of Old City Square is the monument to Jan Hus, a work in Secession style by Ladislav Saloun. In the imposing group of sculptures,

inaugurated on 6 July 1915 on the 500th anniversary of Hus's death, the reformer is surrounded by his followers and by a group of Bohemians, exiled after the Battle of the White Mountain.

A short distance away, in the crowded Staromestské Námestí, the atmosphere changes. Frequently, and rather unimaginatively, described as the "heart of Prague," this square is a magnificent architectural space in which each building has a life of its own but co-exists in rare harmony with the various styles of its neighbors. Just as all the surrounding streets converge on the square, visitors and citizens alike gather here to breathe in something of the unique, unmistak-

able atmosphere of Prague. Crowded one against another, the tall buildings create a symphony of pale and bright colors, in contrast with the dark, severe, tones of the stone town hall and the Church of Tyn, and the whiteness of the Church of St. Nicholas. The vast central space of the square is almost overwhelmed by the dramatic monument to the martyr Jan Hus that successfully evokes the works of Auguste Rodin.

95 The animated complex of the Old City Town Hall and the monument to Jan Hus form the backdrop to traditional dancing, performed by dancers wearing multi-colored costumes in Bohemian folklore. Jugglers and clowns also perform in the square, to the delight of children.

96 left The late Gothic porch of the Town Hall and Tower with the astronomical clock is decorated with flower motifs and figures, sculpted by Matej Rejsek. Both the porch and the window of the entrance hall date back to the period of Vladislav II Jagiello.

96 top right Above the Renaissance window of 1520 in the Kríz House, which today houses the civic marriage registry office, is the coat of arms of Staré Mesto, with crowned lions and towers, adopted by the city of Prague in 1784.

96 bottom right The "Minute House," embellished with 18th-century graffiti with mythological themes, was the last part to be joined to the Town Hall in 1886. In the building, also called "The White Lion" for its corner sign, lived the family of the famous Prague writer Franz Kafka.

The Town Hall, the symbolic monument of Staré Mesto, is an heterogeneous and suggestive complex of buildings. Founded in 1338, thanks to the concession of John of Luxembourg, in the Volflin da Kamen house (i.e. the building in the corner), a tower was added in 1364 and in 1381 the elegant oriel-windowed chapel was built by Peter Parler. The Gothic portal with sculptural decoration by Matej Rejsek, and the beautiful window date from the reign of Vladislav Jagiellon. In the atrium, the mosaics dedicated to Princess Libuse and the Slavs were executed to designs by Mikolás Ales. The inscription *Prague Caput Regni*, "Prague Capital of the Kingdom," sparkles on the baroque gateway of the Kriz house, a later addition embellished with a Renaissance-style window. Above it is the coat of arms of the city. The last two buildings incorporated into the town hall were, in the 19th century, the "House of the Cockerel" and the "House of the Minute."

97 The Renaissance home of the merchant Kríz, painted pink and perhaps the work of Benedikt Ried, is part of the Old City Town Hall. The large window, topped by the inscription "Prague Capital of the Kingdom" is outstanding.

98 left An unusual view of the Old City Square shows, on the left, the Town Hall Clock Tower and, in the background, the Church of Saint Mary of T'yn.

98 right The large 15th-century astronomical Town Hall clock, is the work of the master clock-maker Mikolá of Kadan and the astronomer Jan Sindel, but its extraordinary mechanism was rebuilt in 1490 by Hanus Ruze. The clock is flanked by a skeleton and the allegorical figures of Lust, Avarice and Vanity.

99 left and top right
The Gothic stone house
of Volflin of Kamen,
acquired by the
citizens in 1338, was
the first seat of

Prague's Town
Council. The square
tower was added in
1364 and the chapel
with its bow window by
Parler in 1381.

99 bottom The Town
Hall ceiling is decorated
with plant motifs, with
the Old City coat of
arms and scenes from
Prague's history.

The late Gothic George
Room, with remains of
15th-century wall
paintings and the Great
Meeting Hall are
outstanding.

The most unusual feature and principal attraction of the Staromestská radnice is the complex astronomical clock dating from the beginning of the 15th century. The clock is divided into three sections: the central area features two circles and indicates the position of the sun and the moon in the zodiac (in line with the geocentric theories of the time), the current time in Roman numerals and Old Bohemian time (calculated from sunset to dawn and visible in the external circle) indicated in Arabic numerals. Below is a circular calendar (1866) by the great Czech painter Josef Mánes, with medallions featuring the signs of the zodiac set around the Prague coat of arms and rural scenes symbolizing the months. As each hour is struck, the upper part of the clock, the most intriguing section, is the setting for the slow passage of a number of polychrome statues: the apostles, Death, the Turk, Vanity and Cupidity.

The square's other great monument is the gothic church of the Madonna of Tyn erected in its present form in 1365. Acting as a counterpoint to Saint Vitus's cathedral, up until 1621 this church was the center of the Bohemian reformist movement. Here, King George of Podebrady received communion under the two species (both bread and wine). At his behest the facade was decorated with a gold chalice, an Utraquist symbol, later melted down to provide the metal for the statue of the Madonna that replaced it. The interior of the church, was rebuilt in the Baroque style, with magnificent altars and pictures by Karel Skréta. Tycho Brahe, the Danish astronomer at the court of Rudolf II, was buried here in 1601. St. Mikulá's on the east side of the square is an imposing church of Gothic origins, its current Baroque appearance being the work of Kilian Dientzenhofer (1689-1751). While the white facade features fine Rococo statues by Antonin Braun, the interior decorations create a fantastic space enclosed by balconies, cornices and tribunes that is among the most successful in the whole of Prague. The dome boasts an extraordinary fresco depicting the life of St. Mikulá's by Peter Asam the Elder. The wings to the magnificent stage of Staromestské Námestí are its thirty houses, declining all of the city's various architectural styles. Beginning from the east side, the Goltz-Kinskych palace, an opulent Rococo ediface built by Anselmo Lurago to a design by K. I. Dientzenhofer, is flanked by the Gothic "House at the Stone Bell." The Church of the Madonna of Tyn is faced by the school of the same name with Gothic arches but rebuilt in the Venetian Renaissance style, and the Neoclassical "At the White Unicorn's." The north side features the Art Nouveau building of the Ministry of Commerce, decorated with a mosaic and other figures. On the opposite side of the square, on the facade of the beautiful Storch house is a Neo-Renaissance fresco of *St. Wenceslas on his charge*r. "At the White Horse's," with its Romanesque basement dating from the 12th century, was rebuilt in the late Gothic and Baroque styles. There is an unusual 16th-century marble sign "At the Stone Ram's" or "At the Unicorn's:" a young girl depicted alongside a ram in a naïve representation of the mythical Aries. Still within the Staromestské Námestí district, the old and evocative Melantrichova Ulize leads to Kozná Ulize which boasts one of Prague's most important Renaissance buildings, "The House of the Two Gold Bears." Zelezná instead boasts a graceful Gothic bow-window, the only original part of the Karolinum, the university founded by Charles IV.

100 top left The Baroque style with its rich ornamentation, has left evident traces on the urban fabric of Prague.

100 center left St. Nicholas's was founded in the 13th century by German traders and transformed, 1732-35, to a plan by Kilian Ignaz Dientzenhofer.

100 bottom left The Ministry of Trade was designed in 1898 by Osvald Polivka. The front is oddly decorated by the figures of two firemen.

100 top right In a lane near Old City Square stands the house called "Two Golden Bears." Its porch was added in 1590, to a design by Bonifaz Wohlmut.

100 bottom right "Storch House" stands

out for its fresco of Saint Wenceslas, carried out to a design by Mikolá Ales. It is also called the "Stone Virgin" house.

101 The T'yn Church, which appears in the background behind the monument to Jan Hus, is a Gothic building, with three naves and three presbyteries, built from 1365. Where the golden effigy of the Virgin Mary now shines, one stood the chalice, the symbol of the Utraquists.

102-103 The bourgeois houses in the southern part of Old City Square have poetic names, deriving from their old decoration: "The Storks," "The Blue Star," "The Red Fox." On the facade of the latter, however, now appears a golden Virgin with Child.

105 top right The late-Gothic Powder Gate or Tower was so called in the 17th century because it was used as a gunpowder store. It was built in 1475 for Valdislav II by the famous architect Matej

Rejsek, inspired by that on the Charles Bridge, by Parler. The tower, the start of the "coronation route" is 65 meters high, and its abundant decoration includes the effigies of several Bohemian kings.

Returning to the Old Town square, the true hub of the entire quarter, one can take Celetná Ulice, one of the oldest streets in Prague that takes its name from a kind of bread baked in the Medieval period. Most of the Baroque houses lining the street retain Romanesque or Gothic foundations. The unusual "House at the Black Madonna" (No. 24), dating from 1912 and designed by the architect Josef Gocár is fascinating for its Cubist architecture, anticipating Art Deco and other more modern trends. The Powder Tower is instead one of the 13 gateways to the Old Town from which the "coronation route" led up to the castle. Built in the late-Gothic style and dating from the mid-14th century, the tower was important because it rose near the now lost court of Wenceslas IV. The name derives from the fact that it was used as a gunpowder store.

104 The two large groups of sculpture at the sides of the dome of the Town Hall House, Humiliation and the Rebirth of the Nation, are the work of Ladislav Saloun.

105 top left The large dome of the Town Hall House was built between 1905 and 1906 on the land where the old Royal Palace once stood.

105 bottom left Alongside the majestic building of the Town Hall House stands out the old Powder Tower, one of the few remains of the ancient Prague fortifications, dating back to the Gothic period. It was Wenceslas IV, in the 14th century, who decided to establish his residence in this place, the arrival point of an important trade route.

105 center right In Revolucní, alongside the Town Hall House, rises this splendid building with its facade in Secession style, one of the many which characterize the Old City. The little tower which overlooks it, with its typical Gothic roof, testifies to the noble lineage of its inmates.

105 bottom right The statue of the black Virgin Mary adorns the house of the same name in Celetná Street, one of the few in Cubist style existing in Prague. The building, with its staggered entrance and the versatility of its surfaces, was built in 1911-12 by Josef Gocár. Today it hosts the Museum of Czech Art and Czech Cubism.

106 top In front of the National Museum stands the most famous, significant statue in Prague, dedicated to the patron saint of Bohemia, Saint Wenceslas.
The square of the same name has acted as a setting for dramatic, important events in the country's history, such as the suicide of Jan Palach in 1969 and, twenty years later, the protest march against the repressive police methods, which led to the Velvet Revolution.

The New Town was founded by Charles IV in 1347 when Prague already boasted over 50,000 inhabitants (the majority merchants and artisans) and was one of the largest urban centers in Europe. The lively Na Príkope, one of the Prague citizens' favorite haunts, was created in 1760 by covering the moat surrounding the bastions of Starè Mesto (hence the name "On the Moat"). It leads onto Václavské Námestí, the symbolic Wenceslas Square that has played such an important role in the history of Prague. It was thus named in 1848 during the revolution as an affirmation of Czech identity and in 1918 saw massive demonstrations in support of national independence. It was here in the August of 1968 that the citizens of Prague tried to stop the Soviet tanks and here that, a year later, Jan Palach committed self-immolation in the name of liberty. In 1989, Wenceslas Square was also at the heart of the "Velvet Revolution," with rallies attended by upwards of a million people. The large, elongated square (60 meters broad and 750 long) was originally a horse market. It appears to be under the constant gaze of the equestrian statue of St. Wenceslas surrounded by other patrons of Bohemia (1912), standing in front of the National Museum. Built in the neo-Renaissance style to de-

106 center The four flight of the grandiose staircase of honor, in the National Museum, leading to the Pantheon, is striking for the sumptuousness of its ornamentation, inspired by Renaissance style and embellished with marbles and stuccoes.

106 bottom The Pantheon of the National Museum has a large staircase, overlooked by a dome, with rich multi-hued marble decoration and effigies of celebrated exponents of Czech art and thinking.

106-107 This evocative night view shows Wenceslas Square with the National Museum, a neo Renaissance building, designed by Josef Schulz to celebrate the Czech nation. Founded in 1818 on the initiative of the patriots, it was supported by eminent cultural exponents and completed in 1890. The Museum hosts collections of national history, archaeology, mineralogy, anthropology, and an enormous library.

signs by Josef Schulz (1885-1890), this building boasts grandiose and sumptuous marble interiors, a fountain decorated with allegorical statues symbolizing Bohemia, the Elba and the Vltava and a main staircase with four flights leading up to the Pantheon. Below the dome of this great hall stand effigies of illustrious Czech cultural figures. Most of the buildings surrounding Václavskè Námestí date from the end of the 19th century and represent an attractive sampling of various architectural styles. The Koruna Palace, for example, reflects the influence of eastern civilizations with its Babylonian style, the

Europa Hotel is one of the best conserved examples of the Prague Secession style, the Wiehl House, designed by the architect of the same name with graffiti decoration and frescoes on the facade inspired by Bohemian history, is a successful neo-Renaissance pastiche and the Lucerna palace, once frequented by celebrated musicians such as Saljapin and Toscanini, was designed by and once belonged to the grandfather of the current president of the republic, Václav Havel.

107 top Wenceslas Square, one of the three in the New City, is a link with the Old City.
It was originally called Horse Market Square and two scaffolds and a pillory used to stand there. The square with its elongated shape (60 by 750 meters), is lined with fine houses and the National Museum.

107 bottom One of the most tragic events taking place in Wenceslas Square, sacred to the civic conscience of the people of Prague, was the dramatic suicide of the student Jan Palach, who set fire to himself in protest against the Soviet invasion and the repression of the Prague Spring. Today, immediately in front of the statue of Saint Wenceslas, stands the monument to the victims of the totalitarian regime.

108-109 From the Moldau we have a fascinating view of the National Theater, with its theatrical blue roof studded with golden stars. The building is particularly significant for the Czech people, because in mid-18th century Prague performances in the national language could only very rarely be staged.

108 bottom, 109 top left and 109 bottom right In 1878 Frantizek Zenisek painted an allegorical triptych of the finest moments in Czech art, a work which frescoes the vault of the hall of the theater.

109 bottom left The National Theater has two large auditoria: the New Theater, built in the late Seventies by Karel Prager, and the old one, whose ceiling is decorated with allegorical figures representing the arts, by Frantisek Zenisek. The pictures shows one of the frescoes.

To reach Karlovo Námestí, Novè Mesto's other great square, one crosses Jungmann Square with Cubist lamppost by Matej Blecha and the 20th-century Adria Palace in the Venetian Renaissance style, the first home of the Lanterna Magika theater where Vacláv Havel's Civic Forum met. The National Theater on Národní Trída, designed by Josef Schulz to replace a building destroyed by fire shortly after opening, a domed roof that resembles a turquoise sky scattered with stars and facades that are all different to each other. The principal facade is enlivened by an elegant loggia decorated with statues of Apollo and the nine Muses. The interior

was decorated by the leading Prague artists: the allegories of the seasons in the ladies' boudoir and the red and gold stage curtain were the work of Voytech Hynais, while Mikolás Ales was responsible for the lunettes in the great foyer inspired by themes from Smetana's *My Country* cycle. The National Theater's Nová Scéna, built in glass and concrete by Karel Prager, today houses the Lanterna Magika, an internationally famous theater.

110 right *The National Theater is the country's leading stage, where the works of the major national composers are performed, such as Smetana and Janácek. One of Smetana's operas, Libuse,* dedicated to the legendary founder of Prague, officially inaugurated the theater in 1883, after its reconstruction. *Many stars of ballet and opera have appeared on the stage of the National* theater, as well as numerous famous companies, with unforgettable performances; from the Nutcracker *(above) to Mowgli (center) and* The Barber of Seville *(below).*

110-111 The historic auditorium, reconstructed like the rest of the building after the fire of 1881, has an imposing curtain, the work of Vojtech Hynais, representing the origin of the theater.

110 top left One of the most popular ballets with the people of Prague has always been Giselle, *the charming, dramatic tale performed for the first time in 1841 at the Paris Opera House by the choreographers Jules Perrot and Jean Corelli, to music by Adolphe Adam. On that occasion the leading ballerina was the Italian Carlotta Grisi.*

110 center left and bottom Avant-garde performances have also been staged in this theater, as may be seen in the picture above of the ballet dedicated to Isadora Duncan, and below, a restaging of Carmen. *The Prague audience is always happy to pay due homage. Besides, theater, music and culture in general have always been daily fare for the sophisticated people of Prague, who* have often found fuel for their patriotic feelings in art. It was no coincidence that Mozart spent the most exciting periods of his career in Prague and Franz Kafka wrote and set his most important works in the city. The Bohemian capital is also the center of the most famous school of mime in the world and the leader of the Velvet Revolution was a playwright: Václav Havel.

110

Karlovo Námestí is Prague's largest square and, ever since its foundation by Charles IV, it has been one of the New Town's most important spaces. Originally a great livestock, herring and coal market, the emperor ordered a wooden tower to built on the square, subsequently replaced by a chapel. One a year the crown jewels were exhibited here.

In the mid-19th century the square was laid out as public gardens with statues of celebrated personalities and today is a tranquil oasis with its own particular appeal. A large building occupies the northern part of Karlovo Námestí, the Nové Mesto town hall where demonstrators demanding the release of Hussite prisoners and led by Jan Zelivesky were responsible for the first, bloody "defenestration of Prague." Founded in the 14th century and altered on a number of occasions, the palace retains a 15th-century Gothic tower with the coats of arms of Novè Mesto, and a hall from the same period with two naves that is frequently chosen for wedding ceremonies.

Close to the square, at 11 Kremencova, is one of the most famous and characteristic of Prague's pubs, U Flek°u where the famous Flekovskylezák beer is produced and consumed (in the attractive courtyard-garden during the summer).

112-113 Karlovo Námestí, or Charles Square, so called in honor of its founder, Charles IV; is today a quiet green area in the city center. The old cattle market was in fact replaced by a park with statues of Czech writers, poets and scientists, a veritable oasis of peace in the heart of Prague.

113 The New City Town Hall is a pleasing neo-Gothic building, altered several times in its long, complex history, which began at the turn of the 14th and 15th centuries. It still has its fine Gothic tower of that period, which overlooks the northern part of Karlovo Námestí.

113

114 top left Yehuda ben Bezalel (1520-1609), called Rabbi Löw, for 36 years the head of the Talmudic School, and then supreme Rabbi of Prague, is the author of 15 philosophical-religious studies and himself features as a character in literary works. According to one legend, he created the Golem, the legendary artificial man, and his tomb is still venerated today.

114 top right From the 17th century the tomb stones have become larger to contain detailed information of the life and merits of the dead person. This richly decorated stone, dated 1628, is that of Hendela Bassavi, the wife of the leading Jew in Prague, who was raised to the nobility.

Of the Jewish neighborhood, another of Prague's historic districts, all that remains are a few monumental buildings and the cemetery; they are concentrated in a circular area just a few hundred meters across but evocative of one of the most significant chapters of the city's multiethnic history. A Jewish colony had already been established in Prague in the 10th century, at the foot of the castle, while later two communities of Jews of western and eastern origins were confined on the right bank of the river and eventually amalgamated. Victims of the *pogroms* that from the Medieval period besmirched the whole of Europe, they found protection from sovereigns such as Otokar II. With an edict published in 1254 Otokar guaranteed the Jews freedom of worship, conceded privileges, curbed anti-Semitic violence and forbade enforced baptisms. In 1782 Josef II of Hapsburg conceded civil rights to the Jews and the quarter was named Josefov in his honor. In 1850 the ghetto became the fifth official quarter of Prague, but the extremely unsanitary conditions of its squalid alleys and crumbling buildings led to it being rebuilt, with the wholesale demolition sparing only a few synagogues. The legendary ghetto, a magical and fantastical place, the backdrop to Gustav Meyrink's novel *The Golem* set in the Prague of Rodolf II, thus disappeared. The center of what remained of the quarter, the most incredible site with its strange, mysterious beauty, is the ancient cemetery dating back to the 16th century. As the land available was restricted and the Jewish religion forbids the violation of graves, the tombs were stacked one on top of another in as many as twelve strata, forming that poetic jumble of stone that makes it unique. The 12,000 or so gravestones, scattered amidst the perfumed elder shrubs, boast a wealth of figured inscriptions and symbols relating to the families, names and professions of the deceased. Among the most famous is the Renaissance-style grave of Rabbi Löw where visitors leave pebbles and notes expressing their desires, and that of Hendela Bassevi, the wife of Prague's leading Jew, elevated to noble rank in the 17th century.

116 top left In the former House of Ceremonies of the Funeral Confraternity, built in 1906, we may admire a collection of invaluable manuscripts and prints.

116 top right The Maisel Synagogue was built at the end of the 16th century by Rabbi Mordechai Maisel, Rudolph II's financier, and rebuilt in neo-Gothic style in the years 1892-1905.

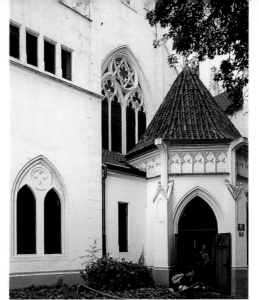

116-117 The neo-Moorish interior of the Spanish Synagogue is inspired by the Alhambra at Granada. The temple was built in 1867-68 to a design by V. I. Ullmann.

117 center left The Pinkas Synagogue, dating back to the 15th century, has a fine architecture in Flemish Gothic style. Today it is a monument commemorating the 77,298 Bohemian Jews exterminated by the Nazis: their names are inscribed for eternal memory on one of the walls.

117 bottom left In Jeruzaemsá Street, near Na Prikopé, is situated a strange building the Jublinejní Synagogue. It is constructed in a composite style, joining Moorish and Secession elements. It was built between 1905 and 1906 by the architect Stiassny to replace three synagogues destroyed at the end of the 19th century.

117 top right We have the first mention of the existence of a Town Hall in the Ghetto in 1541, although the Jewish Community had had administrative and legal autonomy for some time. The present one was built between 1570 and 1577 on the initiative of the Mayor, Mordechai Maisel.

Close to the entrance of the old cemetery stands the 17th-century Baroque Klaus synagogue with its vaulted ceiling decorated with stucco-work. It contains ancient manuscripts and collections of traditional and liturgical objects from the Jewish community. In the adjacent House of Ceremonies, built in the neo-Romanesque style, there is an exhibition of drawings by the children of the Terezin concentration camp. The Pinkas synagogue (1479) features an austere hall with Gothic vaults, trans-

formed into a monument to the Czech victims of the Jewish Holocaust: the names of the 77,297 people who never returned from the camps are inscribed on the walls. The oldest and most important monument in the Ghetto is the Old-New Synagogue (1270-75), one of the first in Europe and built in the Gothic style with two naves and a pulpit and lectern protected by a wrought iron grille. While this temple has been open for worship continuously, the 16th-century High Synagogue has only recently been restored and reopened for religious ceremonies. It once contained a priceless collection of embroidered synagogal textiles. The Maiselova synagogue commemorates Rabbi Mordechai Maisel, a wealthy financier who, during the reign of Rudolf II, obtained privileges for the Jews on the condition that he left half of his fortune to the sovereign on his death. In 1591 Rudolf himself conceded a permit for the building of the synagogue but it was destroyed in the great fire that swept through the Ghetto in 1689. It was rebuilt in the neo-Gothic style and today houses a collection of precious liturgical. On the corner of Maiselova stands the Jewish town hall, rebuilt in the late Baroque style after another fire in 1754. The tower, equipped with a bell, is a privilege conceded by Ferdinand III in recognition of the contribution made by the Jews to the defence of the city against the Swedish troops in 1648. In that period, in fact, only Catholic institutions were allowed to erect bell towers.

Leaving the Ghetto and crossing the beautiful streets lined with Secession-style buildings, among the most important of Josefov's ancient monuments is St. Agnes's Convent, founded in 1234 by the sister of Wenceslas I. This was one of the first Gothic buildings in Bohemia and now, after being restored, houses the National Gallery's collection of 19th-century Czech art. On the banks of the Vltava stands a magnificent complex in the neo-Renaissance style, designed at the end of the 19th century by the architects Zitek and Schulz, and re-named the Rudolfinum in honor of Crown Prince Rudolf of Austria who committed suicide at Mayerling. The home of the Prague philharmonic orchestra and the setting for major musical events, among the various concert halls is the splendid Dvorák Hall, surrounded by elegant colonnades and boasting a precious Rieger organ. Another neo-Renaissance building, situated behind the old cemetery, houses the Museum of the Decorative Arts and was again designed by Josef Schulz. The facade is decorated with relief sculpture symbolizing the crafts.

120 top left Saint Martin's Rotunda was also founded by Vratislav II, who intended to make the fortress the center of his new kingdom. With its original walls and pseudo-Romanesque porch this is the only pre-medieval building surviving in the area.

120 top right This 19th-century neo-Gothic porch belongs to the Church of Saints Peter and Paul, founded around 1070 by Prince Vratislav II and, at the time, the second religious building in the Premyslid kingdom. The two twin spires of the church, added in 1902, dominate the Vysehrad district.

In order to enjoy a wonderful panoramic view of Prague and the Vltava valley and to visit the site of the city's legendary origins, one has to climb the verdant slopes of Vysehrad. Little remains of the tortured history of the citadel, home of the Premyslids and defensive bulwark of the city together with the castle, but abandoned before being rebuilt by Charles IV. The old Romanesque rotunda of St. Martin's, a vestige of the fortifications, and the monumental gateways Leopold, Tabor and Cihelná are still standing. The Romanesque church of Saints Peter and Paul, built at the behest of Vratislav I, has been heavily altered over the centuries, but its two modern towers (1902), looming over the fortress are by now distinguishing features of Vysehrad. To the south of the church extends the park where the 20th-century statues by Josef Myslbek review ancient Czech history by way of the most significant or legendary figures such as Princess Libuse and her husband, the ploughman Premysl. The cemetery of Medieval origins is particularly evocative and was embellished by A. Wiehl at the end of the 19th century with a portico in the neo-Renaissance style featuring painted vaults. The cemetery contains the graves of Prague's favorite sons, including the painter Alfons Mucha and the composers Smetana and Dvorák. The Pantheon, or Slavin, the "place of glory," is dedicated to these personalities.

121 bottom The park
contains four
grandiose groups of
statues by the sculptor
Jodef Myslbek, created
in the years 1889-97.
The subjects are

inspired by old Czech
legends. In this picture
we see the two heroes
Záboj and Slávoj
fighting courageously,
and triumphing over
foreign usurpers.

121

SECESSION, THE FLORAL STYLE

A mong the various artistic trends characterizing the architecture of Prague, of particular importance is the local variation on Art Nouveau, known by the Austrian term of Secession style.

Coming into being towards the end of the 19th century and developing through the first decade of the 20th, the new style harmonized particularly well with existing styles in Prague, acting as something of a counterpoint to the magnificent Baroque architecture and ornamentation that predominate in the city. An immense statue such as the *Hercules* by Mathias Braun in the Clam-Gallas Palace and a bestiary dominated by the proud lions of Bohemia, are balanced by the dancing female figures of Ladislav Saloun and the mysterious owls, bird-icons of the style.

Art Nouveau was a modern aesthetic movement that, at the turn of the century, spread from Paris to influence the architecture of many European cities and was taken up in all forms of fine and applied art. The style comprised a subtle, sophisticated interplay of structure and decoration that aimed at an ideal stylistic unity.

An important role was played by the use of new techniques and materials such as iron, which lightened structures and became a decorative element of facades, or colored glass which helped dilate spaces and surfaces with its unique lighting effects.

122 left The monumental Koruna House, by the architect A. Pfeiffer, is unmistakable with its characteristic massive corner tower, surmounted by a stylized tower. The ornamental relief, of Babylonian inspiration, are by Suchard and Stursa.

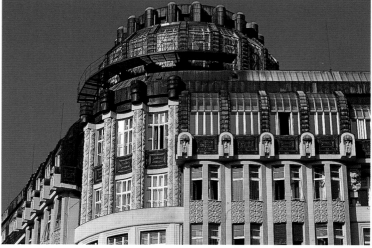

112 top right The use of lunettes and frescoed fronts is characteristic of the houses in old Prague.
Each house, for reasons linked to their family histories, or for inscrutable reasons, is often associated with a clear definite symbol: in this case a relief featuring spring.

122 bottom left Many Secession building face onto Wenceslas Square, fine examples of the various phases of this style which has left a particular mark on the city.
Alongside the typical floral facade of the Hotel Europa we may in fact find buildings where the geometric phase dominates.

123 The front of the former Firemen's Insurance House of Firemen in Staromestké Námestí, designed by Osvald Polívka, is decorated by the mosaic The Apotheosis of Prague by Frantisek Urban. The capital is represented in female garb, while several noblemen pay tribute and the Castle forms the setting to the scene.

While the walls were decorated with variously colored ceramics and mosaics, stained glass succeeded in modifying the quality of the light, intensifying or diffusing it according to the tones, transforming the atmosphere of the interiors. In accordance with modern sensibilities and the new social circumstances, the new style intended to break with the pomposity of 19th-century architecture, with its meaningless and labored eclecticism, and to sever ties with a past that offered little in the way of fertile stimuli. It was, in fact, a veritable "secession" in which architects, along with other artists, painters, sculptors and furniture makers, were able to give free rein to their imaginations. At the end of the 19th century Prague had a population of 400,000 and had witnessed the intensification of the Czech national renaissance. 1891, the year of the Exposition marking the Jubilee of the Kingdom of Bohemia, offered the city the opportunity to renew itself in accordance with the new aesthetic canons and to free itself from a degree of provincialism with respects to Vienna and the great European cities. It was no coincidence that the first major Secession-style buildings such as the Palace of Industry and the Hanavsky pavilion were erected within the grounds of the celebrated exhibition. A reduced scale copy of the Eiffel Tower was actually built on the Petrín hill while the city plan was subjected to radical changes inspired by the boulevards and arrondisements of Paris.

The Central Station (1901-1919), named in honor of the American president Woodrow Wilson and designed by Josef Fanta, boasted an audacious dome and two decorated lateral towers whilst its interior featured Art Nouveau elements in the form of magnificent ceramic mosaics, sculptures and frescoes. This is one of the few examples of public architecture in the Secession style constructed in Prague.

Early in the 20th century entire areas of the New Town and Josefov were razed to the ground to make way for edifices, above all residential buildings, inspired by the new aesthetic canons. Wenceslas Square that from the second half of the 19th century became the political and commercial heart of the city, features some of the most interesting examples of the Secession style, including the Peterkuv House (No. 2) dating from 1889-90 and designed by Jan Kotera, a pupil of and assistant to Otto Wagner. Whilst this work is fairly sober, the Hotel Europa from 1903-06 is striking for the richness of its facade which abounds in

decorative details, colors and gilding. The nymphs supporting the lantern at the top are by Ladislav Saloun. The interior has survived virtually intact, with the café frescoed by Lád'a Novák and the restaurant featuring its original furniture and light fittings. Alongside rises the slim facade of the Hotel Meran which features an attractive floral mosaic. Facing the Europa stands the imposing Lucerna palace, the first reinforced concrete building to be erected in Prague. In close-by Vodickova Street stands one of the masterpieces of the great architect Osvald Políva, virtually a manifesto of the Art Nouveau style. This is the Novak House (No. 2), a felicitous combination of colored glass and metal. The facade is adorned with a magnificent, delicate mosaic by Jan Preisler with allegorical representations of Commerce and Industry. Discreet and sophisticated tones are a feature of the Prague Secession style. At the bottom of Wenceslas Square, the Koruna Palace (1911-1914), with its massive corner tower surmounted by a crown and featuring Babylonian influenced relief sculptures by Sucharda and Stursa, represents a particular phase of the style. Here begins the extremely lively Na príkope which boasts another important work by the architect Polívka, two Secession style buildings with Neo-Renaissance influences linked by walkways. The facades feature mosaics to designs by Jan Preisler and, above the attic, stand allegorical statues by Saloun and Hergesel.

126 left The immense dome of Prague's Central Station, embellished with paintings and sculptures, displays the style of public buildings at the start of last century. The station was designed by Josef Fanta with considerable stylistic restraint: the facade has a strong impact with its two towers and the large central hall, decorated with windows.

126 top right A detail of the semi-circular front, which dominates the Hlahol Choral Club House on the Masaryk embankment, shows in close-up the magnificent mosaic on the theme of song and music. The designer of the building, also embellished by stucco statues and mosaic inscriptions, was the celebrated architect Josef Fanta.

126 bottom right
Osvald Polívka, the architect who left a significant mark on the early 20th-century city, ideated the Neo-Renaissance building of the Bank of Commerce and Crafts in Prikopé Street. This detail shows the sumptuous mosaics of the lunettes, with their historic and allegorical subjects, to drawings by Mikolás Ales.

126-127 Hotel Europa, built between 1903 and 1906, is a successful synthesis of Prague Secession style. Its splendid facade shows a careful balance of all ornamental elements: mosaics and stuccoes, wrought iron and gilding. Inside, the valuable period furnishings have been preserved.

127 Mosaics, one of the main features of Art Nouveau aesthetics, are used in decorating buildings, on which they confer vivacity and a more varied color scheme. This geometric advertising mosaic adorns Lucerna House, designed by Václav Havel, the President's grandfather.

At the bottom of Na Príkope on Námestí Republiky and adjacent to the Powder Tower stands in all its splendor the Obecní d°um (Municipal House), the temple of the Prague Secession style, built between 1905 and 1911 as a multi-faceted cultural center and today restored and returned to its original functions. The building was designed by Osvald Polívka and Antonín Balsánek, in reality the author of the neo-Baroque and neo-Renaissance architecture. The central part of the building from which the two wings depart, has a vast protruding foyer surmounted by a cupola. The allegorical groups of *The People Humiliated* and *The People Revived* by Ladislav Saloun stand either side of the arching pediment on the main façade occupied by the great mosaic *Honor to Prague* by Karel Spillar. The canopy at the entrance to the Municipal House features magnificent decoration in stained glass and wrought iron giving a foretaste of the sumptuousness of the interiors for which the definition "third baroque" was coined. On the first floor the most important areas is the Smetana Hall, thus named for the themes that inspired its decoration such as the allegorical statues by Saloun, *Czech Dance* and *My Country*. The frescoes are by Spillar. This building is of great historical importance as in January 1918 the members of the Czech parliament issued their declaration "of the Three Kings" that demanded independence for the state, while on the 28th of October that same year the

first laws of the Czechoslovak Republic were passed here. Classical concerts have always been held in the building and it is the home of the Spring International Festival of Music. The Reiger Hall boasts notable pictures by Max Svabinsky, with portraits of the principal Czech artists and writers. The precursors of Czech nationalism lent their names to the other halls: the Palacky Hall, decorated with frescoes by Jan Preisler, the Grégr Hall, frescoed by Frantisek Zenisek on the themes of the songs of love, war and death. The masterpiece of the Municipal House is the Mayoral Chamber designed by Alfons Mucha, the leading light of Prague Art Nouveau who came to fame in Paris with his celebrated posters for the theatrical productions of the divine Sarah Bernhardt. The magnificent fresco in the dome tackles the theme of nationalism in an allegorical-symbolic vein. At the center, a great eagle with outspread wings appears to be about to launch itself from the ring of fruit trees around which sit workers in traditional costume. The stained glass, also designed by Mucha, adds further appeal to the overall composition, with light pouring in from three large windows giving onto Republiky Námestí. On the ground floor are the luxurious and elegant French restaurant and café, themselves decorated with stucco-work and frescoes such as Josef Wenig's *Prague welcoming her guests*. Throughout the building the light fittings in glass and precious metals are also original period pieces.

Close to the Municipal House, the Hotel Pariz (1905-1907), one of the most sophisticated in the city, was built in the Gothic Revival style but with strong Art Nouveau influences seen in the plant motif stucco-work and the ceramic mosaics by Jan Kohler inspired by Bohemian folklore. Still within the New Town, along the Masarykovo riverside embankment lined with a sequence of attractive Secession buildings, the home of the Hlahol choir designed by the architect Josef Fanta is worthy of particular mention.

Moving onto Starè Mesto, the Old Town Square features the beautiful monument to Jan Hus, the work of Saloun, set against the backdrop of the fire-fighters' Insurance Company Building (by the architect Polívka), now the home of the Ministry of Commerce. These two Art Nouveau works act as an ideal introduction to Parízská

Ulice, Prague's foremost boulevard and a succession of elegant buildings decorated with cupolas and pediments, towers and turrets. Bow-windows, floral and zoomorphic motifs, bas-reliefs, ceramics and magnificent examples of wrought-iron-work are also features of the adjacent Maiselova, Siroká and Kaprova streets (at No. 11 on this last there are notable stylized female figures in ceramic), built after the destruction of the Ghetto. Alongside one of the surviving Jewish temples, the Old-New Synagogue, is a fine example of the sculpture of the period, the expressive, sorrowful *Moses* by Frantisek Bilek. Parízská Ulice extends along the iron bridge dedicated to the writer Svatopluch Cech, the only one in Prague in the Art Nouveau style. The three-arched bridge, with four 17-meter columns surmounted by statues of Victory, has richly decorated piers featuring six-headed Hydra, bronze festoons and medallions representing Prague. It forms an almost symbolic link to the

130-131 This window of 1931, created by Alfons Mucha for the Cathedral of Saint Vitus to the theme of the lives of Saints Cyril and Methodius, is a perfect example of late Art Nouveau style. The choice of bright colors (red and yellow) for the center of the composition, matching more subdued shades for the less important parts, is typical of the style of Mucha, who was perhaps the greatest exponent of this artistic expression.

131 top center Many houses built at the turn of the 19th and the 20th centuries, display elements of Secession style, such as the relief of this supple dancing figure, enwrapped in the cloud of her dress, which adorns this house in National Street.

131 top center The Czech Svatopluch Bridge is the only one in Art Nouveau style in Prague and is also an important testimony to early 20th-century industrial architecture. Six-headed hydras with the city coat of arms, statues of Victory and Lucifer, medallions with dolphins and the personification of Prague, festoons and waves, make up its lavish decor.

131 bottom center The facade of Wiehl House, by the architect of the same name, completed in 1896, adds to a neo-Renaissance building a loggia and rich Art Nouveau decoration, some of which is the work of Mikolás Ales.

left bank of the Vltava and the castle. St. Vitus's Cathedral at Hradcany boasts an number of important Secession style works. Among these are the stained glass windows by artists such as Max Svabinsky and Alfons Mucha. The former was responsible for the *Apparition of the Holy Spirit* in the chapel dedicated to St. Ludmilla, whilst the latter, with the window dedicated to Saints Cyril and Methodius (1931), created one of the masterpieces of the late Secession.

130 Known as Jugenstil in Germany, Sezessionstil in Austria and Bohemia, as Modernista in Spain, and Liberty or Stile Floreale in Italy, Art Nouveau has brought together multiform artistic expressions and a great number of architects. One of the best-known of those working in Bohemia was Josip Plecnik, who designed the entrances to two houses overlooking the second and third Castle courtyard (illustrated here). His other works include the restoration of part of the south gardens (the so-called "Rampart Gardens"), a project which he achieved in the Twenties.

131 bottom Another detail reveals the refined elegance of the decoration of the famous Hlahol Choral Association House. One of the stories has little balconies decorated with stucco figures, always linked to the theme of music and singing, gracefully holding crowns in their hands.

INDEX

PHOTOGRAPHIC CREDITS

136 The towers of Saint Mary of Tyn, in Staromestské Námestí, are unmistakable for their sumptuous bright spires.

The church, founded by John of Luxembourg and built by Peter Parler starting from 1380, was the main Hussite church in Prague.